# BODILY SENSATIONS

# STUDIES IN
# PHILOSOPHICAL PSYCHOLOGY

*Edited by*
## R. F. HOLLAND

# BODILY
# SENSATIONS

by

## D. M. ARMSTRONG

LONDON
**ROUTLEDGE & KEGAN PAUL**
NEW YORK: HUMANITIES PRESS

First published 1962
By Routledge & Kegan Paul Ltd
Broadway House, 68-74 Carter Lane
London, E.C.4

Printed in Great Britain
by Lowe & Brydone (Printers) Ltd
London, N.W.10

Second impression 1967

# CONTENTS

v

# CONTENTS

# ACKNOWLEDGEMENTS

I AM conscious of a great debt to Gilbert Ryle's article 'Feelings', published in the *Philosophical Quarterly* in 1951. It was the starting-point for my own investigations. Some of my views on bodily sensations were presented at the Philosophical Psychology seminar at Melbourne University, conducted by Dr. A. C. Jackson, in 1960. His tireless unwillingness to let anything I said pass unscrutinized helped me to become clearer about many things. A number of other philosophers at different Australian Universities have been so kind as to read through, and comment on, various drafts of the monograph. Some of their very helpful suggestions are acknowledged in the text. My wife went through the final draft with the greatest care and suggested many improvements in style, as did the editor of this series.

D. M. A.

*University of Melbourne*

CHAPTER ONE

---

# TWO SORTS OF BODILY SENSATION

MY object is to give an account of the nature of *bodily sensations*. The word 'sensation' is used in different ways, but to speak of 'sensations' in common talk is often to speak of bodily sensations. They may be divided into two classes. Sensations of warmth, pressure, motion, distension, etc., form one class. Aches, pains, itches, tickles, erotic sensations, and so on, form the second class.

I draw the distinction between these two sorts of bodily sensation in the following way. A bodily sensation (indeed, any sensation) demands the existence of a sentient being who has the sensation. But in the case of the first class we can distinguish between warmth and a sensation of warmth, pressure and a sensation of pressure, motion and a sensation of motion. For warmth, pressure or motion can exist in the absence of sentient beings. However, we cannot make the same distinction between pain and a sensation of pain, or an itch and a sensation of itching. For a pain *is* a sensation of pain, and an itch *is* a sensation of itching.

Although it is quite natural to say that aches, pains, itches, tickles, etc., *are* sensations, it is somewhat unusual to speak of an aching, itching, tickling or painful

1

sensation. Somebody who did so would probably be understood to mean that his sensation was qualitatively a little unusual, although predominantly aching, itching, tickling, or painful in nature. This is explained when we realize that to speak of an ordinary ache (say) as an aching sensation is to speak pleonastically. In speaking of an ache we are already speaking of a sensation. But in speaking of warmth or pressure we are not necessarily speaking about sensations. So if we *want* to speak of sensations of warmth or pressure we must explicitly add the word 'sensation' (or the word 'feeling').

Let us call sensations of warmth, pressure, motion, etc., *transitive* bodily sensations, and let us call such sensations as aches, pains, itches and tickles *intransitive* bodily sensations. The distinction is a preliminary one, and later we will see that it is not deeply grounded in the nature of things. But it will serve for the present.

In a book *Perception and the Physical World* (Routledge and Kegan Paul, 1961) I spoke of what I have just called the intransitive sensations as *sensations proper*. This now seems to me to be very misleading, because what I have just called the transitive sensations have an equal claim to be spoken of as sensations.

Now one thing is obvious about both sorts of bodily sensation: they are closely connected with perception by touch, and, still more closely, with perception of our own bodily state. We shall begin, therefore, by discussing these forms of perception in Chapters 3 to 6. This will enable us to advance an account of the transitive sensations immediately in Chapter 7. The intransitive sensations give rise to much more difficult problems, and Chapters 8 to 14 will be devoted to making preliminary points and criticizing certain theories of the nature of the intransitive sensations. Only in Chapter 15 will we be ready to advance a positive theory of the intransitive sensations.

The account of tactual perception and perception of our own bodily state requires to be prefaced in turn by a brief consideration of the distinction between *immediate* and *mediate* perception. This will be the business of the next chapter.

# CHAPTER TWO

# IMMEDIATE AND MEDIATE PERCEPTION

I HAVE discussed the distinction between immediate and mediate perception elsewhere.[1] But the distinction is so important for our present purposes that repetition is inevitable. I shall ignore tactual and bodily perception for the time being, and concentrate on drawing the distinction for the other senses, beginning with sight.

If we consider perception, *as opposed to misperception*, we can say (tautologically) that it is perception of some objective state of affairs. But in the case of sight, at any rate, we can draw a distinction between the objective state of affairs that we see *immediately*, and the objective state of affairs that is only seen *mediately*. Suppose that I am looking at a cat. The only thing that I can see *immediately* is something having a certain complex shape and colour. The perception of this object *conveys* or *suggests* to me (in a perfectly automatic way) that there is a cat in front of me. So to say 'I see a cat' is to talk the language of *mediate* perception.

It may help to understand the distinction here if we

[1] *Perception and the Physical World*, ch. 2.

consider the possibility of an object which has *exactly* the same shape and colour as one side of a cat, but which is not a cat at all. Suppose that we perceive such an object, and, as a result, we think we are seeing a cat. We would be mistaken, and yet at the same time we could fairly say that it was not our eyes that had deceived us. In *some* important sense, we were not subject to *visual* illusion. But suppose we think we are seeing a thing with a certain shape and colour, yet there is in fact nothing at all there. In this case we *must* have been subject to visual illusion, our eyes must have deceived us.

The only properties of objects or events that are immediately perceived by sight are: colour, light and shade, shape, size, motion, and spatial relations. These may be called the *visual sensible qualities*. On occasions, of course, such properties of objects are only mediately perceived by sight—suggested by what is immediately perceived. The question may then be asked whether there is always a sharp dividing line between those visual qualities of objects that are immediately perceived and those that are only suggested. And it seems that the answer is that there is no sharp distinction, that immediate perception may shade off into mediate perception. But this does not prevent us from making a distinction between the two.

We go on to a more familiar point. We can talk about what we see at a particular moment; but we can also talk about what we *seem to see*, or what *appears to be seen*, at a particular moment. To use a single word, we can talk about the way things *look* to us (using 'look' in its visual sense). Now very often these idioms are used to make *tentative* perception-claims, to express a tentative judgment that we are seeing a certain state of affairs. But we *can* use them in a purely phenomenological way simply to report what seems or appears to be seen, to report the way things look to us, abstracting from any belief or knowledge of the actual physical situation.

Suppose now that we speak about what we seem to see, in the phenomenological sense of the phrase, but we restrict ourselves to the *immediately* seen. Instead of saying 'I seem to see a cat' we shall say only 'I seem to see a thing of a certain shape and colour'. I think that giving such a phenomenological report is what is meant by philosophers who speak of 'describing our visual sense-impressions'. At any rate, this is the sense I shall give to the phrase 'visual sense-impressions'. We must, of course, beware lest we be led by the phrase into adopting without argument some further *theory* of the nature of sense-impressions. In particular, we must not be led by the substantive 'sense-impression' into the unthinking assumption that sense-impressions are a sort of object.

Two important points about sense-impressions may be mentioned. In the first place, it seems that statements that simply 'record our current sense-impressions' are *incorrigible* for the person who makes such a statement, at the time he makes the statement. He cannot be mistaken about such statements, at any rate in a straightforward way. (I am being dogmatic here, because a full discussion of the point would be a very extended one.) In the second place, it seems that sense-impressions can be more or less *determinate*. If I glance casually at something coloured blue, then it may be that my visual sense-impression will be describable only as an impression of a blue surface, and not as an impression of a surface of a determinate shade of blue. In the traditional example of the speckled hen, our visual impression may be of a surface having an indeterminate number of speckles. (If we deny that sense-impressions can be indeterminate, we shall have to accept the still more curious conclusion that they can have features of which we are not aware. For the description of the impression in a determinate way may be quite beyond us.) It is important to notice that our visual sense-impressions may be very indeterminate indeed. If a small object goes past my face very quickly, then the only possible description of my impression may be that it was an impression of something going by very quickly. The visual experience may be as vague as that.

We now leave sight, and consider hearing. Here, too, we can distinguish between what is immediately and what is mediately heard. 'Hearing a car', for instance, is obviously mediate auditory perception. The only immediate objects of hearing are sounds, and so sounds are the only auditory sensible quality. (It may be that we should add spatial relations between sounds, but this is a difficult question, not to be easily decided. I leave it aside here.)

As well as talking about what we hear on a particular occasion, we can also talk about what we seem to hear on a particular occasion ('the way things sound to us'). And we could speak about what we seem to hear in a purely phenomenological way, abstracting from anything known or believed about what there is to be heard. If we speak about what we seem to hear, in this phenomenological sense of the phrase, but restrict ourselves to the *immediately* heard, we can introduce the notion of auditory sense-impressions. Instead of saying 'I seem to hear a car' we say only 'I seem to hear a certain sort of noise'. Statements recording our current auditory sense-impressions are incorrigible for us, and auditory sense-impressions may be more or less determinate.

The immediate objects of the sense of taste are tastes. We can distinguish between the actual taste of a thing, and the way it tastes to us on a particular occasion, whether or not it really has that taste. In this way we can introduce the notion of gustatory sense-impressions.

Notice, however, that this distinction between real and apparent taste is not as important to us as the corresponding distinctions in the case of vision or even hearing. In the case of sight and hearing we mark our sense of the importance of the contrast by using different words. We contrast what we *see* with the way things *look*, we contrast what we *hear* with the way things *sound*. But we say: 'I can *taste* something bitter'; and also 'It *tastes* bitter to me'.

Smell requires no independent treatment. The remarks made about taste apply equally to smell.

# CHAPTER THREE

# IMMEDIATE PERCEPTION BY TOUCH

FOR all other forms of sense-perception besides seeing, hearing, tasting and smelling we employ the word 'feeling'. No doubt this is the reason, as W. C. Kneale suggests, why there is the doctrine of the five senses.[1] We speak of only one further sense, because we have only one further word. Nevertheless, it will be convenient to distinguish between at least two sorts of sense-perception covered by the word 'feel': perception by touch and perception of our own bodily state. (For convenience, I shall call the latter 'bodily perception'.) These two sorts of perception are not cut off from each other with a hatchet; indeed this is very far from being the case. But a useful preliminary distinction can be made between the two.

In the case of sight, sound, taste and smell, there are sense-organs *naturally associated* with these forms of perception. We see *with* our eyes, hear *with* our ears, taste *with* our tongue and smell *with* our nose. I deliberately use the vague phrase 'naturally associated', because it is not clear that we treat statements like 'I see with my eyes' as logically necessary. It is true that we do not treat them as assertions of

[1] *Philosophical Quarterly*, Vol. I, 1950–1, 'Sensation and the Physical World', p. 116.

empirical fact either: they hover between necessity and contingency because we have not decided for or against creating an analytic connection between 'seeing' and 'having eyes'.

Now in the case of touch, we have no specialized organ of perception like the eyes, ears, tongue and nose, but nevertheless we do speak of perceiving *with* portions of the body. We feel the roughness of the material with our hand, the heat of the water with our toe, the hole in a tooth with our tongue. So the body generally, or the surface of the body, could be described as the organ of touch.

But bodily perception is distinguished from all other forms of perception by having no organ of perception naturally associated with it. When I feel the heat of my hand, the motion of my limbs, the beating of my heart or the distension of my stomach, and do not feel these things by exploring my body with another portion of my body, there is no natural answer to the question 'What do you feel these states of your body *with*?'

In touch, then, we say we feel with something; in bodily perception there is nothing we say we feel with. This serves as a mark to distinguish the two. Our present concern is with touch.

Can we draw the same sort of distinction between immediate and mediate perception by touch that we have already drawn in the case of sight, sound, taste and smell? I think it is clear that we can. If I put my hand into a basin, and then withdraw it saying 'Hot water', we can certainly say that the *heat* of the water is immediately perceived by touch. But it seems that I do not immediately perceive by touch that it is hot *water*. At best, immediate tactual perception only informs me that it is a hot *liquid*.

It seems, in fact, that we can draw up a list of *tangible sensible qualities* to correspond to the visual, auditory, gustatory and olfactory sensible qualities. *Prima facie*, we can immediately perceive by touch that an object is hot or cold, rough or smooth, sticky or slippery, wet or damp or dry, heavy or light, hard or soft, that it is exerting or not exerting pressure, and that it has a certain size, shape, position and state of motion. All these qualities have at least a claim to be considered tangible sensible qualities.

It seems, furthermore, that whatever is *immediately* perceived by touch is in direct contact with the sensitive portions of the body. (As the word 'touch' itself indicates.) When I feel a stone with a walking-stick I do not think it can be claimed that my perception of the presence of the stone is immediate. What I feel immediately is the movement of the stick's handle against my hand. It may be thought that the perception of *radiant* heat is an exception here: that when I feel the heat of a radiator I immediately feel the heat of an object that is at a distance from my body. But is my immediate perception a perception of anything more except the heating up of my own body (which is bodily, not tactual, perception) or a perception of the heating up of the air in contact with the skin? This may be contrasted with sight. Sight does give us (*pace* Berkeley) an *immediate* perception of things-at-a-distance.[1] But there seems to be no corresponding immediate perception of heat-at-a-distance.

[1] I have argued this point in *Berkeley's Theory of Vision*, Melbourne University Press, 1960.

11

However, it must be admitted that the distinction between what is and what is not immediately perceived by touch is not as clear-cut as in the case of sight, sound, taste and smell. In many cases there may be a considerable element of linguistic decision in saying just where immediate tactual perception ends, and mediate perception begins. I think this is especially evident in the perception of *shape* by touch.

But if the notion of immediate tactual perception can gain any foothold, so can the notion of *tactual sense-impressions*. Illusions of touch are not very common, but they can occur. Lukewarm water can feel hot if the hand is cold, the wind feels chillier than it really is if I am in a fever. Two compass points sticking into my back can feel like only one, a pencil put between two crossed fingers can feel double. A hole in my tooth can feel larger than it really is, when explored by the tongue. After wearing a hat for some time, it may still feel as if I am wearing a hat even after it has been taken off. (This last example is interesting, because it is an instance of a *tactual after-image*—an illusory tactual perception succeeding to a veridical tactual perception. And, unlike some visual after-images, the illusory perception is a *simulacrum* of the veridical perception.) It is therefore possible, however unusual, to talk about the way things feel to us by touch in a purely phenomenological way, abstracting from whether things are in physical fact as they feel to be.

So if we talk about the way things feel to us by touch in this phenomenological sense of 'feel', but if we restrict ourselves to the *immediately* felt, we may be said to be describing our *tactual sense-impressions*.

12

The concept of a tactual sense-impression will, of course, inherit any imprecision that there is in the distinction between what is, and what is not, immediately perceived by touch. But, granting this, it seems to be a coherent concept, and a true parallel to the concept of visual, auditory, gustatory and olfactory sense-impressions.

Sight is the most precise of the senses, but even in the case of sight we noticed the possibility of visual sense-impressions being more or less indeterminate. And although touch is seldom *illusory*, our tactual impressions are generally very much less *determinate* than our visual impressions. (Consider the difference between determining the shape of an object by sight and by touch.) Perhaps it is the comparative vagueness of the impressions gained by touch that accounts for the absence of a sharp distinction between immediate and mediate perception by touch.

# CHAPTER FOUR

# THE RELATIONAL NATURE OF PERCEPTION BY TOUCH

I SHALL now try to establish that all immediate tactual perception involves perception of a relation holding between our body and objects in contact with it. In order to have a standard of comparison, however, let us first ask whether this is the case in immediate *visual* perception.

If we consider sight, it seems that we can distinguish between immediate perception of size, position and motion, on the one hand, and the immediate perception of shape, colour, light and shade, on the other. In the case of size, position and motion, part of what is immediately perceived by sight in normal circumstances is a relation between our body and some other object. Things are often seen as bigger or smaller, taller or shorter, than our body; or, to be more precise, than *our body qua visual object*. Again, things are often seen as near or far off, to the left of or to the right of, above or below, our body, and as moving in relation to our body. I do not say that this perception of a relation to our body is invariably present, but it is certainly frequent.

This relational element in the visual perception of

size, position and motion, together with our tendency to assume that in any change it is the environment rather than our body that changes, explains the occurrence of certain simple sensory illusions. As we grow up, that is as our body gets bigger, the things in our environment look smaller. If our bodies could expand and contract to a marked degree in a short time, presumably the objects around us would seem to dwindle and to grow in sympathy. When I turn my head or my body, the environment may appear to move. If I am in a fast car, the things my body is approaching may appear to rush towards me.

But this contrasts sharply with the immediate visual perception of shape, colour, light and shade. I do not see a ball as rounder than my head, or a surface as the same colour as my skin. No perception of a relation to my body is involved.

But if we now turn to immediate perception by touch, we find that a perception of a relation between our body and an object seems to be involved in the perception of every tangible property.

We have seen that all immediate tactual perception involves *contact* between sensitive portions of the body, and the things perceived. Now not only is there always such contact, but there is always perception of this contact. Part of what we immediately perceive is that a certain portion of our body is in contact with the object. This is proved by the fact that we can say straight off, without any research, what portion of the body is in contact with the object perceived by touch.

But immediate tactual perception is still more deeply infected by relation, as we shall see if we work through the list of the tangible sensible qualities.

In the case of heat and cold, I think that what we immediately perceive by touch is a *difference* in the heat of the surface of our body and the surface of the object touched. In tactual perception, I suggest, the primary meaning of 'hot' is 'hotter than my body'; the primary meaning of 'cold' is 'colder than my body'. (In its secondary meaning however, 'hot' means 'hotter than my *normal* bodily state', and 'cold' means 'colder than my *normal* bodily state'.)

Here an objection may be made. I can tell that water is hot by putting my hand in it, but this normally involves little or no consciousness of the heat of my hand, or the surface of my hand. So 'hot' cannot have the force of 'hotter than my hand'. However, this objection fails to remember that we very often perceive relations between things without any clear perception of the nature of the related things taken by themselves. I may see quite clearly that two things are equal in length, but have no clear idea what that length is. My perception of a difference in heat between my body and the object touched need involve no clear perception of the heat of my body taken by itself.

I must admit, however, that most philosophers with whom I have discussed this point have argued that, as a matter of phenomenology, the heat immediately perceived by touch is perceived simply as 'hot' and not as 'hotter than my body'. I do not know how to settle the argument, and it may be that heat and cold are exceptions to my thesis about the relational nature of tactual perception.

Perception of pressure, which we can take to cover both pressing on, and pulling at, our body or portions of our body, is quite obviously a *perception* of a relation of objects to our body. We feel the pressure as a pressing on, or a pulling at, our body.

Other things being equal, an object feels heavy if it is hard to lift or carry. An object feels light if it is easy to lift or carry. If our body were more powerful, what now feels heavy would feel light.

Hardness and softness, as immediately perceived by touch, are obviously relative to the hardness or softness of our flesh. If we feel a solid object pressing on our flesh (as opposed to the pressure of such things as water or wind) and our flesh giving, that object feels hard. If we had 'greater force and firmness of limbs' [1] we should not say that certain objects feel hard.

In perception by touch, a sticky thing is one that sticks to our skin. A slippery object is one that our skin slides over very easily. The degree of felt roughness or smoothness of a surface is given by the amount of resistance felt when our skin and the surface move in relation to each other, while remaining in contact. If our skin moved more, or less, easily over a certain surface, our judgment of the degree of felt stickiness, slipperiness, roughness and smoothness would necessarily alter.

The immediate tactual perception of size, position and motion quite obviously involves a perception of contact between an object and portions of our body. If our body became very large in relation to our environment, then an object *now* in contact with a relatively large portion of the surface of our body would be in contact with a smaller portion. It is clear

[1] Berkeley, *Three Dialogues*, p. 222, Everyman.

that if this happened the object would feel smaller to us. Felt position and motion require no independent discussion.

We are left with the qualities of wetness, dampness, dryness, and also shape. It is not so obvious that tactual perception of these properties involves any perception of a relation between our body and the object touched. But equally it is not clear that in the case of these qualities we have pure cases of immediate perception by touch.

Let us consider shape first. If we take a simple case where we are purely passive, for instance when a round ball is pressed into our skin, the *immediate* perception of roundness seems to be no more than a perception of pressure-contact between an object and the concavity formed in our flesh. Only if we feel *the concavity in the flesh* can we tell the shape of the object pressing on us. Normally, of course, discovering shape by touch is a matter of active exploration, usually by the fingers or perhaps the tongue. But again 'feeling the shape' seems to be a matter of immediately perceiving pressure-contacts between the particular portion of the body employed, feeling the motions that we have to go through to maintain pressure-contact, or feeling the shape the portion of the body employed assumes under contact. So the immediate perception of shape reduces to a mixture of bodily perception and the tactual perception of pressure. The latter is a perception of a relation to our body.

Now to deal with wetness, dampness and dryness. Dryness may, I think, be ignored, because 'dry' is only a negative term meaning 'not wet'. What shall we say about wetness? A thing in a liquid state is a thing that behaves in a characteristic way, a behaviour almost as readily perceivable by sight as by touch. But to the extent that wetness *is* immediately perceived by touch it seems to be no more than a perception of such things as heat or cold, slipperiness, and light contact over a continuous area. All these have been shown to involve perception of a relation to our body. Unless the heat of the liquid touched is exactly the same as the surface of our body, a difference in heat will be noticed over a continuous area. Wet things usually feel somewhat slippery. If a finger is put in water, the water exerts a very gentle uniform pressure over the whole surface of the finger. Such perceptions seem to be all that is involved in the immediate tactual perception of something wet. The perception of dampness is similar. What we immediately feel by touch are such things as the unusual temperature, texture and slipperiness of the damp object.

If this argument is correct, all immediate perception of tangible qualities involves perception of a relation between our body and the tangible object. I proceed to draw some conclusions from this.

In the first place, we said in Chapter 3 that if we are going to talk about an *organ* of touch, we can talk only about the particular sensitive portion of the skin which is in contact with the object perceived. But we now have to recognize that, in tactual perception, the organ enters into the perception in a special way.

We have already seen that some immediate visual perception involves perception of a relation between our body and other objects (for example, perception of size and position). But the relation perceived does

19

not hold between the *organ* of perception and the object perceived. I do not perceive immediately that the object is bigger than my eye, or a long way away from it. I do not see my eye at all, but only *other* portions of my (visual) body, which I can compare with other objects in certain respects. It is the same with sound, taste and smell. Save *per accidens*, I do not hear my ear, taste my tongue, or smell my nose.

But in the case of touch, I do perceive a relation between the sensitive portion of the body and the object in contact with it. I feel that the water is hotter than my finger which implies perception of a relation between my finger and the water. I feel the object dig into my ribs, which implies perception of a relation between my ribs and the object. The 'organ' of perception is itself immediately perceived. So all tactual perception is in a certain sense perception of our own bodily state.

This shows that we were wise to say that tactual and bodily perception are not sharply distinguished. We have already noted that we use the same word 'feel' for tactual and bodily perceptions. We now see that the former involves the latter.

Indeed, we might replace the distinction between tactual perception and bodily perception by the distinction between *transitive* and *intransitive* bodily perception. In intransitive bodily perception our immediate perception is confined to states of the body. This we call 'bodily perception'. In transitive bodily perception we immediately perceive a relationship between our body and something else in contact with it. This is 'tactual perception'.

# CHAPTER FIVE

# THE NATURE OF THE TANGIBLE QUALITIES

THE next proposition I shall try to establish about immediate tactual perception is that, with the exception of heat and cold, all the tangible qualities reduce to *spatial* properties of objects.

Size, shape and motion are themselves spatial properties, and so require no discussion. A *rough* surface is a surface of an object in the solid state, a surface that has some degree of hardness, and a certain *irregular shape*. It is this hard irregularity which ensures that such a surface will not move easily over the skin. A smooth surface differs only in lacking irregularity of shape. So roughness and smoothness can be analysed in terms of the *spatial* properties of surfaces, together with the properties of hardness, and being in the solid state.

A *hard* object is one that does not change its shape, or break up easily (a form of change of shape), under pressure; while a soft object does change its shape easily under such conditions. So hardness and softness are analysable in terms of *shape* and *pressure*. Liquids and solids are distinguished by the different contours that something liquid and something solid assume in various circumstances. (It is a mark of a liquid that it *runs.*) There seems to be nothing involved in solidity and liquidity that does not resolve into spatial properties of objects, unless it be the different contours that liquids and solids assume when *under pressure*. So roughness and smoothness, hardness and softness, being solid and being liquid, involve no reference to anything except spatial properties of objects together with the notion of pressure.

Lightness and heaviness, also, we can give an account of in terms of pressure, in terms of the push or pull of objects on our body or of our body on objects, especially when we lift or carry things.

Can we give an account of pressure in purely spatial terms? In physics, and even in ordinary discourse, we have a concept of pressure that does not always involve some actual happening. But if we confine ourselves to pressure as it is perceived by touch, we can say that it always involves an actual change. What happens is that contact with a material object causes a change in the spatial properties of parts of our body, that is, their shape, size or position. The more heavily a body presses or pulls upon our flesh, the more the body's normal spatial properties are altered. Of course, a weight on my head will cause a different sort of change from the change caused by putting the same weight on my stomach.[1] But a considerable weight on my head will cause a bigger change there than a smaller weight at the same place. Again, sometimes the changes that are involved in the spatial properties of our body are changes involved in *resisting* pressure— the tensing of our muscles, and so on.[2] But the greater

[1] A point put to me by Professor J. A. Passmore.
[2] A point put to me by Mr. G. O'Hair.

the pressure, the greater will be the change in the body necessary to resist it. We do go on to form a more sophisticated conception of pressure, involving no more than a power or tendency to make things move. But pressure perceived by touch is a matter of actual bodily displacement or change. Nor does pressure seem to involve any further element. If a thing in contact with us is displacing a portion of our body, it is pressing upon us. So we can give an account of perceived pressure solely in terms of the perception of change of spatial properties of physical objects.

One difficulty remains. The concept of pressure involves the concept of causation, of one thing making another happen. But can we have *immediate* perception of causal relationship? If we cannot, pressure cannot be immediately perceived. The question is a difficult one, and deserves a more extended discussion than I am able to give it. But I am inclined to say that there is no objection to the immediate perception of causal connection. (And, at the same time, I do not think that this necessarily contradicts a Humean or semi-Humean analysis of the *nature* of causation.) It is simply one of the peculiar features of tactual perception that it gives us an immediate awareness of objects *making things happen* to our body, and our body making things happen to objects.

There remain only such qualities as stickiness and slipperiness. These are dealt with simply. A sticky thing remains in contact with the skin, requiring pushing or pulling to detach it, while a slippery thing is one that moves readily over the skin.

Heat and cold, however, seem to resist this sort of

dissolution. It might be said that heat is simply *temperature*, and that temperature can be identified with the average kinetic energy of the molecules comprising the hot thing, or with the readings given by thermometers. Such an account of heat and cold might reduce them to spatial properties of objects. But it seems a sufficient objection to these identifications to point out that it is an *empirical discovery* that felt heat and cold have anything to do with the movement of molecules or the readings of thermometers.

Again, one might be tempted to say that heat and cold are simply bodily *sensations*. But this will not do, because we predicate 'hot' and 'cold' not only of our bodies, but also of insensitive physical objects. We say that the water in the next room is hot, and we seem to mean by this just what we mean when we say that our body is hot. (I shall return to this point in Chapter 10.)

It seems, in fact, that heat and cold belong in a group with sound, taste, smell, colour and perhaps light and shade. These qualities of objects are traditionally known as the *secondary* qualities (spatial properties being included in the list of the *primary* qualities), and it will be convenient to use this term. But I do not want to presuppose any particular philosophical theory of the 'secondary' qualities. Nevertheless, it does seem that heat and cold belong to this group, however we name it. If my argument has been sound, the tangible qualities include no other secondary qualities.

There is one difference between heat and cold, on the one hand, and such qualities as colour, on the other, that may be noticed. We associate hot things with *activity*: in particular, a hot thing communicates its heat. The other secondary qualities are not like this. It is true that striking a certain note may shatter a wine-glass, but we certainly do not make the shattering of glass part of our concept of sound. But while this difference between heat and cold, on the one hand, and the rest of the secondary qualities, on the other, does exist, it does not seem to be very important. What has happened, I take it, is that our concept of heat reflects certain very general facts about the world. It is originally a mere teaching of experience that hot things communicate their heat. Later this becomes, or tends to become, part of the essence of heat.

Now if it is true that, with the exception of heat and cold, all the properties of objects immediately perceived by touch reduce to *spatial* properties, then we are faced with a new problem. The problem may be brought out by considering *sight* once again.

It seems that the visual perception of shape, size and motion is only possible because we also perceive light, shade and colour. I cannot perceive by sight that a certain object has a jagged outline (a determination of its shape), without perception of a difference of colour or shade where the object ends and its environment begins. Without this perception of difference in secondary quality there would be no visual perception of the outline. The secondary qualities act, as it were, as *demarcators* of the spatial properties. (To use a word suggested to me by Mr. D. C. Stove.) Visual perception of spatial properties is bound up with perception of secondary qualities.

Now it may seem that the same argument should apply to immediate tactual perception. If we perceive various spatial properties of objects by touch, do we not require perception of non-spatial properties to act as 'demarcators' of the spatial properties? Is not a perception that is completely confined to spatial properties impossible precisely because of the lack of such 'demarcators'? Yet then the difficulty arises that there seem to be no properties immediately perceived by touch that could play the role of colour, light and shade in vision. Heat and cold seem quite inadequate by themselves, for there can be immediate tactual perception without any thermal perception at all. For instance, I may feel a heavy pressure but have absolutely no perception of heat or cold. Now if pressure is simply a matter of changes in the spatial properties of my body caused by contact with some object, there is here no immediate perception of further properties to fill out the perception of spatial changes.

It seems to me, however, that all this dilemma does is to bring out the great difference between sight and touch. If we consider the world *immediately* revealed to sight, we can say that it is something less than the world of *material objects*. It is a world of what might be called 'visual objects'. The shapes, sizes and motions that are immediately perceived by sight are shapes, sizes and motions of these visual objects.

I do not want to be misunderstood here. I am emphatically not saying that in immediate visual perception we are locked up inside a circle of our own sense-impressions. I am using 'perceive' in the sense in which it is *opposed* to misperception, in which it is opposed to the having of mere sense-impressions. The vast majority, if not all, of the visual objects that are the immediate objects of sight are *as a matter of fact* material objects.[1] But that they are material objects is information *not* given to immediate visual perception. (It may be helpful here to consider the case of somebody who has sight, but absolutely no sense of touch or bodily perception. Such a person, it seems, could have the concept of an objective world of happenings. But could he have the concept of a *material* thing?) The nature of the objects immediately perceived by sight, then, is exhausted by these qualities of colour, light and shade. Hence immediate visual perception of spatial properties must be a perception of objects having these qualities of colour, light and shade.

In the case of touch, however, what is perceived to be in contact with our body is not a 'tactual object', but is simply *a material object having certain spatial properties*. If we say that in immediate vision the 'demarcator' of shape, size and motion is a thing of colour, light and shade; then perhaps we can say that the 'demarcator' of the spatial properties in immediate tactual perception is a material thing. Then there seems no need to find other qualities immediately

[1] It is difficult to find an uncontroversial example of a visual object that is not as a matter of fact a material thing. The example of rainbows may be suggested. But Professor J. A. Passmore has pointed out to me that even a rainbow might be said to be material: an expanse of moisture through which light is striking. I am also unwilling to use such examples as mirror-images, because I hold that they are *illusions*, a view I have argued for in *Perception and the Physical World*.

27

perceived by touch to act as 'demarcators' of the spatial properties perceived.

But here a difficulty may be raised. What is a material object? It is very tempting to say that what makes a material object *material* is that it can exert pressure on our body, and that our body can exert pressure on it. A material object can make my body move through contact, and my body can make it move.[1] (This would help to explain the close connection that many philosophers have thought to exist between the concepts of material object and causality.) A visual object, *qua* visual object, cannot exert pressure on my body, nor can I exert pressure on it. (I cannot make a spot of light move, except by manipulating its material source or the material thing on which the spot falls.) Now if a material object is simply 'that which can exert pressure on us, and on which pressure can be exerted' we are not really providing any 'demarcator' for the tangible qualities in saying that they are perceived as qualifying a material object. For pressure, we have argued, can be analysed in terms of the spatial properties of objects. So immediate perception by touch gives us nothing but spatial properties, and no perception of any 'demarcator' of these properties.

Perhaps this conclusion just has to be accepted. No doubt the spatial properties perceived by touch must have a demarcator, but perhaps touch fails to elicit any knowledge of the intrinsic nature of the demarcator of these properties (with the possible exception of

[1] The importance of these criteria for our concepts of a material object has been pointed out to me by Mr. D. L. Gunner.

heat and cold). I do not really think that there is anything paradoxical here *unless we are hypnotized by the model of sight.* So it is an important conceptual point about immediate perception by touch that it is a perception of material substance; but this does not necessarily mean that material things are the 'demarcators' of the spatial properties perceived by touch. For it seems that 'being material' is to be defined in terms of the spatial properties immediately perceived by touch.

But if this is so, it may be further objected, it is not true that the immediate objects of sight can never be immediately perceived to be material objects. For the properties that make a thing material are reducible to purely spatial properties, and any spatial property can be immediately perceived by sight. But this objection fails to remember that the concept of pressure, which is the central concept for the understanding of the concept of a material thing, involves the notion of *causality,* of one thing making another thing happen. Now immediate visual perception may involve seeing one thing coming into contact with another, and, succeeding to this, changes in shape and position of the two things. But this will not be an immediate perception of *pressure,* because there will be no immediate perception of the *causal transaction.* Only touch yields immediate perception of pressure, and so only touch yields *immediate* perception of material objects.

It may be remarked in passing that sound, taste and smell resemble sight rather than touch in not involving immediate perception of something material. This conclusion is obvious in the case of sound and smell, but may seem more dubious in the case of taste. But here it must be remembered that the tongue is not only the organ of taste, but is also a very sensitive organ of touch. When we taste something, we generally *feel* the material object that has the taste. But this does not prove that the *immediate* object of taste is *a material object having a taste*, rather than simply *an instance of a certain sort of taste*. And the following consideration suggests that the latter is the sole object of immediate gustatory perception. If a very small amount of substance having a certain taste is introduced into my mouth I may taste that taste, even though I cannot tell whether there is anything material in my mouth.[1]

If this difference between touch on the one hand, and sight, sound, taste and smell on the other, has been made out, then light is thrown on some ideas about touch that it is natural to entertain. There has always been the suggestion in the air—Plato attributes it to the Giants in the *Sophist*, and it becomes explicit doctrine in Condillac, for example—that touch is *the* sense that gives us access to reality. Vision may be more detailed and precise, but somehow it fails to come to grips with things.

We can now understand this line of thought. Touch

[1] We must distinguish between (i) an impression as of a bitter taste in my mouth, which may or may not correspond to objective reality; (ii) an actual bitter taste in my mouth; (iii) a material substance in my mouth having a bitter taste. The distinction between (ii) and (iii) is obscured because, *as a matter of fact*, it is only material substances that have tastes. But we can imagine this not being so. Just as we can imagine everybody hearing a sound that has no material source at a certain place, so we can imagine everybody tasting the same taste at a certain place but having nothing material in their mouths.

is the sense that gives us 'access to reality', because even in immediate tactual perception the *object* of perception is something material. Of course, there is something mistaken in this line of thought also, for in all cases the immediate objects of perception are objective things. Not everything in the world that is real need be a material object. But it is easy to think of material objects as *the* real things;[1] and once we do this, touch becomes the only access to reality.

We may now sum up the contentions put forward about touch in the last three chapters.

(i) It is possible to draw a distinction, even if a rough one, between what is and what is not immediately perceived by touch. It is therefore possible to draw up a list of *tangible qualities*; properties of objects that are immediately perceived by touch.

(ii) Since tactual illusion is possible (although rare), we can talk about what feels to us to be perceived by touch, abstracting from whether or not there really is anything to be perceived, and restricting ourselves to the *immediately* perceived. In this way we can introduce the notion of tactual sense-impressions. Such a concept will inherit any vagueness that there is in the distinction between immediate and mediate tactual perception.

(iii) All immediate tactual perception involves perception of a relation between our body and something

[1] Mr. D. L. Gunner has pointed out that the tendency to treat material objects as *the* real things is connected with the role that material objects play in the fulfilment of our most primitive and pressing desires—our desires for food and drink. Only something material could assuage hunger or thirst, a mere 'visual object' could not possibly do so.

in contact with it. Tactual perception might even be called 'transitive bodily perception'.

(iv) With the exception of heat and cold, all the properties of objects immediately perceived by touch reduce to spatial properties.

(v) Unlike immediate visual perception (or hearing, tasting or smelling), immediate tactual perception is a perception of *material* objects. This is not to deny that the other senses give us an immediate perception of events in the objective world.

---

# CHAPTER SIX

# PERCEPTION OF OUR OWN
# BODILY STATE

WE can now consider perception of our own bodily
state. By bodily sense we perceive that our legs
are moving, that our head is turned, that our arm is
behind our back, that we are keeping our balance, that
our body-temperature is up, our ears cold, our stomach
distended, our gut full, our throat dry, our heart beating, our muscles tensed or relaxed, and all the other
things that we discover about the current state of our
body without recourse to sight, hearing, taste, smell
or touch.

As has already been pointed out, perception of our
own bodily state is not naturally associated with any
*organ* of perception. There is nothing I am conscious of
using to tell me that my temperature is up or my hand
behind my back.

There is a further peculiarity of bodily perception:
the objects of this sense are private to each perceiver.
Nothing mysterious is meant by this: attention is
simply being called to the fact that bodily perception
informs each of us what is going on in his own body,
and nobody else's. Our fields of view can overlap, we
can hear the same sound, smell the same smell, taste

and touch the same object. But I cannot feel the motion of your limbs or the distension of your stomach by bodily perception. (Of course, I can discover these things by *touch*.) In respect of this sense we really are locked up inside our bodies. Or, to put it in a more cheerful way, we have privileged access to information about our own body. Indeed, it is one of the marks that makes us call a certain object 'our own body' that we can perceive some of the things that go on in it, in a way that we cannot do with other bodies.

Can we draw the same distinction that we drew in the case of touch (even if a little uncertainly) between immediate and mediate perception? I think we probably can, but the line of division is even harder to indicate exactly than in the case of touch. If I say I feel the fullness of my stomach, this seems to be the language of *mediate* perception, reading into what is immediately perceived a certain amount of anatomical information. But what is *immediately* perceived in this case? Perhaps nothing but an outward pressure in the middle region of the body. To take another example: when I say I feel the straining of a muscle, what is immediately felt? Perhaps there is a vague perception of internal stretching.

The difficulty in drawing a sharp line between what is and what is not immediately perceived by bodily perception is, I think, due to the great vagueness and imprecision of this sense. The information it gives us is even more imprecise than the deliverances of tactual perception. Sometimes the perception is nothing more than a perception of 'something-or-other going on in a certain portion of the body', with no possibility of specifying the 'something-or-other' more definitely.

When tired, I sometimes feel a very tiny 'tic' immediately under the eye. What is immediately felt? Nothing I think, except the rhythmical occurrence of a motion in a small area of the flesh. The nature of the motion is completely indeterminate.

But although bodily perception is so vague and imprecise, it is seldom erroneous. If it felt as if there were a tic beneath our eye, we should be astounded to be informed that in fact no unusual motion was going on in that place. If our stomach felt distended, we should be astounded to learn that the stomach was not distended at all, nor was there any unusual outward pressure being exerted in that part of the body.

Nevertheless, sensory illusion is possible, even with bodily perception. We can feel hot when we are not hot. When we come ashore after some time at sea we feel as if we are keeping our balance in the normal way, although in fact we are swaying slightly, in the same way that we learnt to sway at sea.[1] Amputees report that it still feels to them as if they had the missing limb, and they may say it is in one position rather than another. (We may ignore here, as irrelevant for our present purposes, their reports of aches, pains and itches in the phantom limbs.)

The cases of amputation are especially interesting. We may distinguish between *sensory illusion* on the one hand, and *hallucination* on the other, in the following way. In sensory illusion, an object *that really exists* perceptually appears to have some characteristic that

[1] We do, however, correctly perceive *that there is swaying going on*. But because of our tendency to assume that, in any change, it is our body that does not change, it feels to us as if the *ground* were doing the swaying.

in fact it does not have. In hallucination, however, we seem to perceive an object *that is not there at all*. Now, if we adopt these definitions, it is clear that feeling hot when we are not hot, for instance, must be said to be mere bodily sensory illusion; but that feeling a phantom limb is a case of hallucinatory bodily perception.

But even if illusion of either sort did not in fact occur in bodily perception, we could still *imagine* it occurring. We could, for instance, imagine our stomach feeling distended, in the complete absence of any unusual physical pressure in that part of the body. We can therefore *introduce* a sense of the word 'feel.' In this sense of the word, saying our body feels to us to be in a certain state leaves it perfectly open whether or not our body is really in that state. Once we have done this, we can speak about what feels to us to be the case, in this introduced sense of the word 'feels', and further restrict ourselves to the *immediately* perceived. We have then introduced the notion of *bodily sense-impressions*, just as we previously introduced the notion of tactual sense-impressions. The concept will inherit all the imprecision of the distinction between immediate and mediate bodily perception, but, granting this, the concept of a bodily sense-impression seems to be a perfectly intelligible one.

We can conclude our discussion of bodily perception by asking what properties of the body are immediately perceived by this sense.

The answer, I think, is exactly the same as in the case of tactual perception (yet one more indication of the lack of any sharp gap between the two). Except for heat and cold, the properties of our body immediately perceived by this sense are purely spatial properties.

The sort of thing I am aware of in bodily perception is the motion and position of limbs, the position relative to the earth of the whole body, the pressure of one part of the body on another, the stretching of tissue. All these things, it seems, resolve themselves into spatial determinations of the body. Heat and cold are the only exceptions.

What has these spatial properties is a *physical object*: our body. What are immediately perceived are *spatial properties of a particular physical object*. Our body is, indeed, for each of us, the paradigm of a physical object, and it is no accident that the word 'body' can mean either human or animal bodies, or material objects *generally*.

It may be objected that this account of bodily perception has left out the most important thing: bodily *sensation*. But the rest of the book is an answer to this objection.

# CHAPTER SEVEN

# TRANSITIVE BODILY SENSATIONS

OUR discussion of tactual and bodily perception is completed, and with it the introductory part of this book. We can now consider directly the nature of bodily sensations. In this chapter we shall give an account of the *transitive* bodily sensations—sensations of warmth, of pressure, of motion, of distension, etc. The rest of the book will be devoted to the far more difficult problems posed by the *intransitive* sensations.

Talking of the transitive sensations, I suggest, comes to the same thing as talking about bodily sense-impressions, or, in some cases, tactual sense-impressions. When we speak about what we feel by bodily sense (or sometimes by touch), disregarding the question whether what we feel really exists or not, and restricting ourselves further to the *immediately* perceived, then we are speaking of our (transitive) bodily sensations. It is true that to talk about such things as sensations of pressure is rather less *precise* than the stricter rules we have laid down for the expression 'bodily sense-impression' (or 'tactual sense-impression'). Thus, in talking about sensations of pressure, I think there is no clear decision made whether or not to disregard the question of the real existence of what we feel. But ordinary language can afford to avoid this decision, because, as we have seen, illusions of bodily feeling are comparatively rare. Granting this, the 'transitive' bodily sensations are nothing but bodily (or tactual) sense-impressions. To have a sensation of pressure is to feel that a portion of our body is under pressure; to have a sensation of heat is to feel that a portion of our body is hot.

But this identification may be challenged. It may be said that a sensation of heat in the hand is not really an impression as of our hand being hot, but is simply something that we normally *happen* to get when our hand heats up. It gets its description 'sensation of *heat*' simply from the causal conditions of its production. And the same may be said of all the other 'transitive' bodily sensations.

This view may be held in two forms. (i) It may be said that so-called 'bodily perception' is nothing but the having of certain bodily sensations, which we learn to associate with states of our body. On having the sensations, we infer that our body is in a certain state. But taken by themselves the sensations are 'blind', they do not point to any physical state of our body. It would be easy to conceive that what we now call 'sensations of heat' occurred only when one part of our body was pressing on another part with unusual force. Then they would be called 'sensations of pressure', yet their intrinsic nature would be unaltered. Somebody who held this reductive view of bodily perception might go on to take the same view of tactual perception. (This account of tactual and bodily perception is at least suggested by G. J. Warnock in his book *Berkeley*, pp. 47–8.)

(ii) The same sort of view may be held in a less radical form. It may be allowed that there are bodily perceptions of such things as the warmth of a hand or the motion of a limb. But these perceptions are not to be identified with the transitive bodily sensations. The sensations just happen to accompany the perceptions, but are quite distinct from them.

The first view seems thoroughly implausible. If all bodily perception is a matter of having sensations which only suggest to us that our body is in a certain physical condition, then we shall have to offer some account of the way we learn that the sensations are associated with a certain bodily condition. It will be circular to say that we get this information from bodily perception. It will have to be acquired by sight, sound, taste, smell or touch, if touch is allowed. But it does not seem possible that we should acquire the considerable knowledge we have of the states of our own body that accompany 'transitive' sensations in this indirect way.

But even if we take the second, less radical, view, where bodily perception is not reduced to the having of certain sensations; it is still very difficult to say that sensations of heat or pressure are simply phenomena that happen to be produced by heat and pressure. On such a view there is a mere *contingent connection* between sensations of heat and the heat of a limb. But if this is so, it is very mysterious that we have no vocabulary to describe the sensations as they are in their own nature, apart from the conditions in which they are normally produced. Their quality seems to be *exhausted* by the 'conditions of their production', which suggests they are simply *impressions of* heat, pressure, motion, etc.

It is true that there seems to be some phenomenological difference between sensations of heat and pressure, on the one hand, and *kinaesthetic* sensations on the other. As Wittgenstein notices in the *Investigations* (pp. 185–6), the latter are curiously 'transparent'. This suggests that *they* may be simply impressions of the motion and posture of our body, but that sensations of heat and pressure do involve something more.

But it does not seem that there is any important difference here. What happens, I think, is that (i) sensations of heat and pressure are often accompanied by certain *intransitive* sensations (heat by prickling, for instance) which are usually absent in the case of kinaesthetic sensations. (ii) Sensations of heat and pressure arouse affective attitudes much more readily than kinaesthetic sensations.

So I think the identification of transitive bodily sensations with bodily (or in some cases tactual) sense-impressions remains very much the simplest and most plausible account available.

In any case, if the identification is rejected, then some further account of the nature of transitive sensations must be given. It seems that such an account must be very similar to the theories of the nature of the intransitive sensations to be discussed in Chapters 9, 11 and 12. (The intransitive sensations as qualities of the body, as *sui generis* items located in the body, as items not located in the body.) And the arguments that will be advanced against these accounts of the intransitive sensations can equally be turned against similar accounts of the transitive sensations.

# CHAPTER EIGHT

# BODILY SENSATIONS AND
# BODILY FEELINGS

A HARDER task lies ahead: that of giving an account of what we have called the *intransitive* bodily sensations; things such as aches, pains and tickles. Since these are the subject of the rest of this book I shall often refer to them simply as 'bodily sensations' or 'sensations'. Where I refer to the transitive sensations I shall say so explicitly.

Our first problem is to say just what should be included in the class of (intransitive) bodily sensations. The following criterion may be suggested: such a sensation is *located* in some portion of our body (or, in the special case of amputation, in one of the places where the limb would be if we still had that limb). Aches, pains, itches, tickles and tingles may be in any portion of our body. Other sensations have a *restricted* bodily location: we have stitches in our sides, nausea in the stomach, or erotic sensations (characteristically) in the 'erogenous zones'. But we can ask of any bodily sensation: 'Where is it in our body?'

This marks off bodily sensations from what we might call '*bodily feelings*': feeling fresh, feeling tired, feeling faint, feeling sleepy, feeling sick and so on.[1] It makes no sense to ask for the bodily location of our feeling of sleepiness, or feeling of sickness; although such bodily feelings may *involve* having bodily sensations (either transitive or intransitive) which *do* have a bodily location. In some cases the same phrase may refer either to a bodily sensation or to a bodily feeling. A 'feeling of hunger' may refer to pangs in the stomach, and then it is a bodily sensation. But we can feel hungry without having pangs, and that is a bodily feeling.

However, there is a difficulty in using this criterion of bodily location to distinguish bodily sensations from bodily feelings. We might be inclined to say that *dizziness* and *giddiness* are bodily sensations, not bodily feelings; yet that they are not located. The case of dizziness is thoroughly ambiguous. We have some inclination to say it is located in the head, for 'dizzy in the head' is a possible idiom. But I think we also have some inclination to say that dizziness is not located anywhere. At any rate, it is clear that we do not locate *giddiness* anywhere in our body. Yet it is as natural to class dizziness and giddiness with the bodily sensations as with the bodily feelings. For the present we will class them as intermediate cases, and will confine our attention to the bodily sensations that *are* located.

I shall not discuss 'bodily feelings' any further. They involve interesting problems, though not of the same difficulty as those connected with bodily sensations, but we cannot consider these problems here. They have

[1] Cf. Gilbert Ryle, 'Feelings', *Philosophical Quarterly*, Vol. 1, 1950–1, p. 194.

been distinguished only to be dismissed, for our concern is with the intransitive bodily sensations. I shall now go on to examine in turn five theories of the nature of the intransitive sensations, and present objections to each. Finally I shall present a modified version of one of these theories which I believe is more satisfactory. One important question that any such theory must be able to answer is: 'What does it mean to *locate* a bodily sensation?'

# CHAPTER NINE

# INTRANSITIVE SENSATIONS AS QUALITIES

IT is clear that to say I have a pain or an itch or a tingle in my hand is not like saying there is bone or blood in my hand. A bodily sensation is not a material object.

But perhaps we can say that sensations are *sensible qualities* of portions of my body. What sense are they discerned by? Perhaps we shall have to revise our account of bodily perception, and say that by means of this sense we perceive not only spatial and thermal properties of our body, but these 'sensational' qualities also. In a modern psychology text-book on sense-perception (*The Human Senses*, Frank A. Geldard, John Wiley, New York, 1953) the tenth chapter puts together *pressure* and *pain*. The comparison that seems to be implied is that physical pain is a bodily happening, perceived in just the same way that bodily pressure is perceived. However, the obvious comparison is not with pressure, but with the secondary qualities; and, in particular, the only secondary quality discerned by bodily perception: heat. Just as I feel my hand is hot, so I feel my hand is painful or itchy. In each case I perceive a quality of a certain physical object, my hand, by means of bodily sense; the pain or itch is in my hand in the same way that the heat is in my hand. Locating a sensation is like locating the portion of my body that is hot.

We shall now advance a number of objections to this account of bodily sensations. Some of these objections are inconclusive, but others are final.

### (i) *We do not perceive bodily sensations*

We say that we *perceive* the sensible qualities of physical objects or events, that is, that we see, hear, taste, smell or feel them. But we do not say that we perceive bodily sensations. We simply *have* them.

It is true that this argument is not, by itself, conclusive, because we do speak of *feeling* a pain or an itch, and it may then be argued that this is the perceptual sense of the word 'feel'. But whenever we speak of feeling bodily sensations we can substitute the word 'have' without changing our meaning. This is not the case for the perceptual uses of the word 'feel'. 'I feel the heat of my hand' does not mean the same as 'I have a hot hand', for I could have a hot hand without feeling it. But if I have a *pain* in my hand, it seems I must feel the pain.

The only reply to this would be to argue that we can have a pain without feeling it. Now there are certain arguments which might tempt us to say this, but I do not want to discuss these arguments at the moment. So, for the present, let us just note that, unless a distinction can be drawn between having and feeling sensations, we have found a difficulty in assimilating bodily sensations to sensible qualities.

46

## (ii) *Bodily sensations are private*

The sensible qualities of physical objects, it may be said, can be perceived by anybody whose sense-organs are suitably placed, and in a suitable condition. But only I can feel my pain, my itch or my tingle. So they cannot be sensible qualities. Their privacy makes them something else.

But our discussion of bodily perception has shown that this is an invalid argument. It is a fact about bodily sense that it does not extend beyond my own body. I cannot, for instance, perceive the heat of *your* hand by bodily perception. So if bodily sensations are sensible qualities discerned by bodily perception, we may expect that our perception of pain-quality or itch-quality will be limited to our own body also. It is true that I can perceive the heat of your hand by an-other means: by touching. But somebody who wanted to assimilate bodily sensations to sensible qualities could say that all this proved was that heat was a quality immediately perceived by two senses—tactual perception and bodily perception—while pain-quality and itch-quality were immediately perceived by bodily sense only.

## (iii) *Bodily sensations can only qualify the bodies of sentient creatures*

But if bodily sensations are sensible qualities of physi-cal objects, such as hands or scalps, why do they only qualify people's bodies? Sensible qualities such as heat or colour can qualify *any* physical object. It might be replied that it is simply a contingent fact about the world that these sensation-qualities qualify only living bodies. But this only leads to a re-formulation of the objection. Granting this to be so, it must then *make sense* to speak of the sensation-qualities qualifying other objects besides living bodies. Yet this supposition does not seem to make sense. 'There is a pain in that watch' or even 'There is a tingle in my amputated hand' are nonsense.

Nevertheless, I do not think that this third objection is conclusive, because shift might be made to meet it in the following way. The reason why it is absurd to say that there is a pain in a watch, or a tingle in an amputated hand, is that these objects are not present parts of anyone's body. Now, it could be argued, it is a contingent fact that the sensation-qualities qualify the objects they do and not others, but it is *not* a contingent fact that these objects are called people's *bodies*. For one of the things that makes me call a thing 'my body' is the fact that I feel sensations in that thing. I could imagine feeling a tingle in an amputated hand, or even a pain in a watch, but then my concept of my body would tend to expand to include these objects.

## (iv) *Bodily sensations cannot exist unfelt*

The sensible qualities of physical objects can still qualify the objects they do qualify, even when nobody is perceiving them. The wall is white, although nobody is looking at it. The bell rings out, although nobody hears it. The smell lingers in the room, although there is nobody to smell it. The apple is sweet, although nobody tastes it. The surface is smooth, although nobody touches it. My hand is hot, although I do not feel its heat. Just what this shows may be disputed. Phenomenalists, in particular, exhibit a grudging attitude to these possibilities. But there is no doubt that we do attach sense to the notion of an unseen colour, an unheard sound, an unsmelt smell, a smooth surface untouched, bodily heat not felt.

But, it seems, bodily sensations cannot exist unfelt. We may pay little attention to our sensations, we may scarcely feel them, but we cannot dispense with feeling them altogether. If we do not *feel* a sensation at all, then we do not *have* that sensation. This decisively differentiates bodily sensations from sensible qualities.

Now, although this line of thought is so obvious and so attractive, there is one phenomenon that may suggest it is incorrect. It is, as we have already said, possible to pay more or less attention to our bodily sensations. But it is even possible, on occasions, to be so completely distracted by some other demand on our attention that we cease to *feel* a sensation. Yet it is not clear that in such circumstances we cease to have the sensation.

Suppose that I have a headache or an itch, then, provided they are not too severe, other events may solicit me, and I may stop feeling them. Afterwards, when the distraction has passed, I may feel the headache again, or again feel itchy. There are then two considerations that may lead me to say that my head ached, or my back itched, even when I did not feel the sensations. In the first place, it is natural to speak of the headache or the itch that I feel after the distraction is over as being the same individual headache or itch that I felt before the distraction. But where we attribute numerical identity to objects that exist at different times; where we re-identify, as Strawson puts it;[1] it is at least natural to suppose that the object exists continuously between the two times. This means, in the present cases, that we *had* the headache or the itch during the time we were not *feeling* it. In the second place, to talk about my being distracted from something seems to imply that the thing I am distracted from continues to exist. If it ceased to exist, there would be nothing for me to be distracted from.

So when we consider the possibility of being distracted, we do have some inclination to drive a wedge between feeling and having bodily sensations. But it is vitally important to realize what a special case this is. If, for instance, I became unconscious I certainly would not say that I went on having bodily sensations that I did not feel. If I took aspirin, and, as we say, the headache stopped, I cannot entertain the possibility that I still have the headache although I cannot feel it. The existence of an 'unfelt sensation', if we admit the notion at all, seems to be logically dependent upon *distraction*, upon the existence of more pressing demands on the attention. If I am asked to say whether I feel a headache or an itch now, and if I think about the question and return a candid answer of 'No', then I have not got a headache or an itch.

But even where we are distracted from our sensations, we do not feel entirely easy about saying that sensations exist unfelt. We are driven both ways; we are inclined to assent to both sides of the argument. When it is represented to us that sensations can exist only where there is consciousness of them, that their *esse* is *sentiri*, we assent, and draw the conclusion that

[1] P. F. Strawson, *Individuals*, pp. 31–6.

to have a sensation we must feel it. But when we are reminded of the possibility of being distracted from our sensations, we may be drawn, a bit unwillingly,[1] to allow the possibility of having bodily sensations without feeling them.

These conflicting tendencies in our thinking suggest that the true solution will be a compromise between them. I suggest that in cases where we are distracted we should allow that the phrase 'unfelt bodily sensation' has a use, but we should deny that the words 'bodily sensation' have the same force as in ordinary talk about (felt) bodily sensations. An 'unfelt bodily sensation', I suggest, is *a permanent but unfulfilled possibility of feeling a certain sort of sensation*. To say that I have a headache, but that I am not feeling it, is to say that something is engaging my attention, and that if it were to stop engaging my attention, I would feel a headache. But it does not imply that there is a headache going on in any more substantial sense than this. In this way, I hope, we can account for the phenomenon of being distracted from bodily sensations, while still holding to the principle that the *esse* of sensations is *sentiri*.

But what about the arguments that we produced for the existence of unfelt bodily sensations when distracted? Do they not point to a more full-blooded existence for unfelt bodily sensations? I do not think so. After a period of excitement, I may remark that I still have the same headache that I had before the

[1] It is embarrassing to be asked, for instance, whether our sensation did or did not retain exactly the same qualitative characteristics, and the same bodily location, during the period of distraction.

51

excitement. But suppose I have a headache that comes and goes, as some headaches can. I might say 'Here *it* is again', yet not imply that it existed in the interval, even as an unfelt possibility of bodily sensation. For, in the case of bodily sensations, our criteria for numerical identity are not rigid, and we can allow that 'the' sensation leads an intermittent existence. There is still the argument that distraction implies the actual existence of the thing we are being distracted from. But if I am temporarily distracted from my sorrow we *need* not assume that occurrent feelings of grief continue, feelings which I have, but do not feel. There need only be a disposition to have (conscious) feelings of grief when *not* distracted. Why cannot we say the same about bodily sensations?

I conclude, then, that bodily sensations cannot exist unfelt, unless we mean by 'bodily sensation' a mere possibility of having sensations if a current source of attention were to cease being a source of attention. This marks off bodily sensations from the sensible qualities of objects.


### (v) *We cannot be good or bad at feeling bodily sensations*

In his article 'Feelings' [1] Gilbert Ryle argues that in the perceptual sense of the word 'feel' we can be good or bad at feeling, but that we cannot be good or bad at feeling bodily sensations. He goes on to say that in the perceptual sense of the word we can try to feel, and improve or deteriorate at feeling, but that such notions have no application to the feeling of bodily sensations.

[1] *Philosophical Quarterly*, Vol. I, 1950–1, p. 194.

At first sight one may be inclined to reject Ryle's view. One person may certainly be more interested in his bodily sensations than other people are in theirs, and may give them much more attention. And so he may furnish much more detailed *reports* of his bodily sensations than other people can give of theirs. Now what are we to say about such reports? Are we to say he is only much better at putting his experience into words than other people? I think we are strongly tempted to say that there is more to it than that, and that he is actually *better at feeling sensations* than other people are. Once we allow this, we must also allow that the notions of trying to feel bodily sensations, and improving or deteriorating at feeling them, do make sense.

At the same time, however, the reason why Ryle wants to reject the possibility of being good or bad at feeling bodily sensations, trying to feel them, and improving or deteriorating at feeling them, is perfectly clear. If I get better at feeling my bodily sensations, then this seems to imply that *before* I got better there were features of my sensations of which I was not aware. Once again, a wedge would be driven between the *having* and the *feeling* of bodily sensations.

So it seems we must again invoke the account of unfelt sensations given in the previous section. Let us admit the fact that if somebody pays close attention to his bodily sensations he may attribute new characteristics to them that he did not attribute before paying the attention. Let us also admit that this can be called 'getting better at feeling our sensations'. But we shall not admit that this implies the actual existence of unfelt characteristics of sensations alongside the felt characteristics. The newly felt characteristics existed before only in the sense that, if we had paid close attention to our sensations in the past, they would then have had just the (felt) characteristics that they now feel to have.

Of course, if statements about 'unfelt bodily sensations' or 'unfelt features of bodily sensations' were cashed in terms of *physiology* or in terms of *behaviour* then they might be perfectly acceptable as reports of something *actual*. If I forget my pain in the heat of battle, but it is shown that the impulses travelling to the brain do not alter, or if I unconsciously continue to favour the painful place, or rub it unconsciously, we can talk about an 'unfelt pain'. But it will be straining language to call such occurrences unfelt *sensations* of pain.

## (vi) *Bodily sensations cannot be misfelt*

Perception implies the possibility of misperception. We can always conceive of misperceiving the sensible qualities of a physical object. A surface can look green to us when it is not really green, we can seem to hear a noise when there is no noise to hear. We can seem to smell a smell where there is no smell, there can taste to be a bitter taste in our mouth although in fact there is no taste there. Our hand can feel cold to us, although it is in fact not cold.

But if we feel a sensation in some portion of our body, the possibility of error is not present. We cannot say 'My hand feels sore, but perhaps I am mistaken, and my hand is not really sore'. This is a decisive difference between bodily sensations and sensible qualities.

But is it really true that bodily sensations are

necessarily just as they feel to be? Cases may be cited to show that mistake is possible after all. First let us distinguish between the felt location of bodily sensations and their other felt features—such as the quality of the sensations or their intensity. For the moment, let us lump all these other features together and call them the 'qualitative' features of our sensations. We then have two questions: 'Must the qualitative features of our sensations be as they are felt to be?'; and 'Must the bodily location of our sensations be as it is felt to be?' We will consider each question in turn.

Take the following case.[1] Somebody has experienced severe pain in the region of the heart. On describing the nature of the pain to a doctor, he learns that it is a symptom of a serious heart condition. On another occasion he gets a *different* sort of pain in the same place. Is it not conceivable that, on getting this new sort of pain, he may panic, so that at first it *feels to him* as if it is the old pain again? Again, is it not possible, especially if we panic, for a pain to feel to us to be more intense than it really is?

Now I think that these cases do show that we are prepared to allow that there is a 'margin of uncertainty' in the way our sensations feel to us to be. We are prepared to allow uncertainty, perhaps even error, *within limits*. If I feel an intense pain, we *may* be prepared to say that it is not quite so intense as it feels to be. But are we prepared to say that the pain is really very mild, or that it does not exist at all, or is really an itch? (In the case of the sensible qualities of physical objects *complete* hallucination is perfectly possible.)

[1] Suggested by Dr. John Burnheim.

So there remains a distinction between bodily sensations and sensible qualities here. Even if it makes sense to speak of a distinction between the way our sensations feel to be and the way they really are, the gap cannot be a wide one. Our sensations are, of necessity, *much* as they feel to be. But in the case of sensible qualities total error is perfectly possible.

Even so, these examples do open up a gap, however small, between the actual sensation that we have and the sensation we feel to have, which contradicts our earlier conclusion that, in the case of bodily sensation, feeling and having come to the same thing. Now, some of these examples can be dealt with in exactly the same way as in the previous two sections. If my pain feels to be a heart-pain when it starts, but closer attention as it continues shows it not to be this sort of pain, we could say that its felt characteristics had simply changed when we gave it closer attention. The difficult case would be one where we said 'It felt to be a heart-pain, but I now realize that it did not have the right qualitative characteristics *then*.' I am uncertain whether this is a possible case. If it is, we shall just have to modify our earlier conclusion and admit that the having and the feeling of sensations do not coincide *completely*.

Now it seems that the same sort of minor error may be possible about the *location* of our bodily sensations. Close attention to our sensations may lead us to say that they are not quite where they felt to be originally, although it can hardly lead us to say they are in a quite different place. I might decide the tingle was not quite where I originally located it in my ear, but not that it was really in my leg, or even in my cheek.

But there are *other* considerations which might make us admit the possibility of really radical error about the location of bodily sensations. Dentists sometimes tell us that a pain we feel in the lower jaw is 'really' in the upper jaw, in the place where the affected nerve is. When amputees feel pain in the place where their limb would be if they still had it, we may be inclined to say that the pain cannot really be where it feels to be. The pain must really be in the stump. So perhaps we can be *completely* mistaken about the location of bodily sensations.

However, these considerations arouse in us a very ambiguous response. We feel their weight, and at the same time we feel inclined to deny them any weight. They throw us into a small conceptual crisis. When the dentist tells us that the pain is 'really' in the upper jaw, we are impressed by what he says; yet at the same time we are inclined to say that the place *of the pain* can only be the place where the pain feels to be. In the case of the amputated limb, it certainly seems very strange to say the pain is outside our body, and yet, if it feels to be there, how can it really be in the stump?

So these considerations both incline us, and do not incline us, to give sense to the notion of mis-locating our bodily sensations. This is quite different from the location of sensible qualities of physical objects, where we immediately and easily admit the possibility of mistake.

It seems, therefore, that if we take all these considerations together, we must refuse to assimilate the intransitive bodily sensations to sensible qualities of our body perceived by bodily sense. To say my hand is hot means that a certain quality qualifies my hand. To say my hand is hurting does not mean that a pain-quality qualifies my hand. It may be added that our arguments would tell against some more vaguely stated view of bodily sensations: that they are some sort of physical event or happening in our bodies, discovered by bodily perception.

# CHAPTER TEN

# INTRANSITIVE SENSATIONS AS SENSE-IMPRESSIONS (I)

THE collapse of the suggestion that intransitive bodily sensations are sensible qualities qualifying portions of our body leads on to a more plausible idea. We have already argued that the *transitive* bodily sensations (sensations of heat, pressure, motion, etc.) are simply *impressions* of bodily heat, bodily pressure and bodily motion. That is to say, we have identified the transitive bodily sensations with bodily sense-impressions. Why cannot we identify the intransitive bodily sensations with bodily sense-impressions also? 'My hand feels sore' will now be compared with 'My hand feels hot' where 'feels hot' is not taken to imply (or exclude) my hand being hot in physical reality.

If we take this view, we shall find that the objections brought against the identification of intransitive bodily sensations with sensible qualities quite lack force. Instead, we are provided with a number of striking resemblances between sense-impressions and intransitive bodily sensations.

(i) We said that we do not speak of perceiving bodily sensations, but only of having them or feeling them.

But we do not speak of perceiving sense-impressions either, and we do speak of having them, or, in the case of bodily sense-impressions, feeling them.

(ii) We said that anybody could perceive the sensible qualities of objects, but that only I can feel my bodily sensations. Equally, only I can have my sense-impressions.

(iii) We said that if bodily sensations were qualities qualifying parts of our body, it should at least make sense to attribute these qualities to other physical objects. This point requires discussion, because we are now suggesting that bodily sensations are a species of sense-impression, and it does not seem that sense-impressions can qualify, or be located in, my body.[1] So what are we now to make of the 'bodily location' of bodily sensations?

If we consider the totality of our visual sense-impressions at a particular time, we can speak of our *visual field* and of the 'location' of particular visual sense-impressions *within* this field. However, we cannot give the visual field itself a location. In the same way, if we consider the totality of our bodily sense-impressions at a particular time, we could speak of our *body-image* (some psychologists do so) and of the location of particular bodily sense-impressions *within* this body-image. However, we cannot give the body-image itself a location.

Perhaps, then, when we say that there is a pain in our hand, we really mean that our pain-impression is

[1] Although the point will be discussed again later in the chapter.

located in the hand-part of our body-image, just as our visual impressions are located in portions of our visual field. There would then be no question of locating our bodily sensations in a physical object. The fact that we *appear* to do so could be explained when we recall that, because illusions of bodily perception are rare, our body-image generally corresponds exactly to the actual state of our body. Hence, speaking of a sense-impression as if it were located in the physical body is not seriously misleading.

(iv) We said that sensible qualities can qualify objects which are not perceived, but that bodily sensations cannot exist unfelt. We allowed that one could speak of not feeling bodily sensations that one was having, in cases where one's attention was distracted from them. But we suggested that to talk about having un-felt sensations was simply to talk about the bodily sensations one would feel if undistracted.

Now bodily sense-impressions cannot exist unfelt either. And, again, the only exception one might be prepared to make is where one was distracted from them. Suppose, for instance, my hand feels hot to me or my stomach distended, but other matters solicit my attention. Later I realize that I still have the feeling of heat or distension. Here an analysis of such situations in terms of the bodily impressions one would feel if un-distracted seems very plausible.

(v) We were inclined to reject Ryle's view that one cannot be good or bad at feeling one's bodily sensa-tions. Yet at the same time we wanted to deny that this implied that sensations could have unfelt features existing alongside the felt features. So we suggested, once again, that statements about unfelt features of our bodily sensations should be analysed in terms of what we would feel if we gave the task attention.

Such an account would fit in very well with the view that bodily sensations are a species of bodily sense-impression. For it does seem that people can be better or worse at attending to their sense-impressions, yet at the same time one is reluctant to say that sense-impressions can have features of which we are not aware.

(vi) Finally we argued that, while it is possible to misperceive the sensible qualities of objects, it is not possible to mis-feel our bodily sensations. It is true that we had to qualify this second assertion a little. We allowed that feeling our bodily sensations did involve a margin of imprecision, and that error might even be possible within this margin. Careful attention to our bodily sensations may lead us to say that they are not quite as they felt to be at first. It is true also that consideration of certain cases (for example, amputated limbs) may incline us to say that, in the case of the *location* of bodily sensations, even more radical error is possible. But a wide difference remains between sensible qualities and bodily sensations.

Now we should equally want to deny that we can be mistaken about our current sense-impressions, although again we should perhaps be prepared to make certain qualifications. We have already noticed that our sense-impressions may be more or less precise or determinate. Here is the 'margin of imprecision' that we allowed in the case of feeling bodily sensations.

And we might be prepared to admit that *within this margin* we could make errors about our sense-impressions, errors corrigible by closer attention.

It is true that this identification of bodily sensations with bodily sense-impressions fails to explain our half-inclination to say that our bodily sensations may be really located in a *quite different* place from their *felt* location. But perhaps this can be explained by saying that to talk of the 'real' location of the bodily sensation is only to talk of the location of the *cause* of that sensation.

So the identification of intransitive bodily sensations with bodily sense-impressions (just like the transitive bodily sensations) explains many things. It is a conceptual hypothesis not to be lightly rejected. Nevertheless, there remain two serious difficulties which have to be overcome before the identification can be accepted.

### (i) *Intransitive bodily sensations do not correspond or fail to correspond to physical reality*

It is a feature of sense-impressions that they either correspond or fail to correspond to an objective state of affairs. We can say that we are having a visual sense-impression as of something blue or round, but we can go on to ask whether there really is any blue or round physical object corresponding to our sense-impression. We can say that it feels to us as if our hand were hot, but go on to ask whether our hand is in fact hot. But it is quite different in the case of the intransitive bodily sensations. It makes no sense to say that our hand feels sore or feels itchy, and then go on to ask whether it really *is* sore or itchy. 'It feels hot, but is it really hot?' makes sense, but 'It feels sore, but is it really sore?' makes none.

This distinction between bodily sense-impressions and the intransitive bodily sensations might be broken down, or at any rate the nature of the distinction might be elucidated, if a certain very popular view is taken of what it means to attribute sensible qualities to physical objects. This view offers as an *analysis* of the statements 'This (physical) object is round' or 'This (physical) object is coloured blue', the statements 'This object *looks round* and *feels round* (furnishes round sense-impressions) to normal observers under normal conditions' and 'This object *looks blue* (furnishes blue sense-impressions) to normal observers under normal conditions.' We may call this view a *Phenomenalist* account of sensible qualities. It may be, but is not always, combined with a Phenomenalist account of the nature of physical objects themselves. This theory takes a somewhat eccentric view of what it is for a sense-impression to correspond to the sensible qualities of physical objects. Water that feels hot to me is *really* hot if the sense-impressions of normal observers are the same as mine. On this view, therefore, 'correspondence' is really coherence.

Now let us use this analysis of what it is to attribute sensible qualities to physical objects to explain why, when I feel a pain in my hand, it makes no sense to ask if there really is a pain there. It is possible for different observers to have visual or thermal sense-impressions of exactly the same physical object. But our pains, itches, tickles, etc., are confined to our own body. My hand can give me pain-sensations, your hand can give you pain-sensations, but neither of us can have pain-sensations in the other's hand. This is different from the case of colour or of heat: my hand could give you colour-impressions or heat-impressions. That is to say, my hand could look pink or feel warm to you. The result of this *contingent* fact about the intransitive bodily sensations is that it is never possible to make a *survey* of opinion to determine whether a certain object (say, a hand) is yielding intransitive bodily sensations or not. Since, in these matters (it is argued), the distinction between appearance and reality depends upon the result of such a survey, the distinction between 'There feels to me to be a pain in my hand' and 'There really is a pain in my hand' finds no place in our language. (Consider the possibility that tasting was such that no two people could ever taste the same thing. In that case, the ordinary distinction between '*tastes sour to me*' and 'really *is* sour' would never have a chance to get going.)

But suppose that we started to locate pains and other sensations in *each other's* body. Suppose that when I felt pain in my hand, you also felt pain *in my hand*. Suppose further that this sort of thing was pretty general. We would then be in a position to distinguish between 'I feel a pain there', and 'There really is a pain there.' When everybody agreed that they felt pain *at one place*, we would say that there really was pain there; when one person felt pain there, but others did not, it would be apparent pain. Feeling pain (or other intransitive bodily sensation) would be having a species of bodily sense-impression, and there would be a sensible quality 'pain' which 'corresponded' or 'failed to correspond' to this sense-impression.[1]

So, if we accept a 'Phenomenalism of sensible qualities', the intransitive bodily sensations are a sort of bodily sense-impression that, as a matter of empirical fact, the body can furnish only to its owner. If the body could furnish impressions of the same sort to many *different* observers, then the intransitive bodily sensations could be promoted to full bodily sense-impressions, and it would become legitimate to talk about 'sensible qualities' of pain, tickle, itch, etc.

My objection to this ingenious account of the distinction between intransitive bodily sensations and bodily sense-impressions is simply that I cannot accept the doctrine of 'Phenomenalism of sensible qualities'. My reason for rejecting this doctrine is that, when a 'Phenomenalism of sensible qualities' is thought out, the consequence is either a complete Phenomenalism about the physical world, or else a Representative theory of perception. And I believe that both these theories can be refuted. It would take me too long to argue for the latter contention here, but I will say something in support of the former.

[1] In the *Investigations*, 312, Wittgenstein says: 'Let us imagine the following: The surfaces of the things around us (stones, plants, etc.) have patches and regions which produce pain in our skin when we touch them . . . In this case we should speak of pain-patches on the leaf of a particular plant just as at present we speak of red patches.' But surely 'pain-patch' here would mean 'patch that produces pain *in us*'. Yet when we speak of a red patch we do not mean 'patch that produces red in us'. I think that Wittgenstein should have taken the weirder case where we all feel the pain *in the leaf*.

66

Since our knowledge of the physical world comes from perception, we have to determine whether or not we are normal observers and whether or not conditions of perception are normal, *by perception*. But this means discovering certain *sensible qualities* of the observer, and of the situation in which observation is made. So 'This object is blue' becomes 'This object *looks blue* to normal observers under normal conditions'; which in turn becomes 'This object *looks blue* to observers having certain sensible qualities, in a context of objects having certain sensible qualities.' But then we shall be forced to give an account of the qualities of the observer and the conditions of perception, in terms of further normal observers and normal conditions. So, in order to avoid a vicious infinite regress, we shall ultimately be forced to give an account of the sensible qualities of observers and the conditions of observation *purely* in terms of actual and possible sense-impressions. We are then faced with the alternatives of making the physical world something 'hidden' behind the sense-impressions we have of it, or else of giving an account of physical reality purely in terms of sense-impressions. And both these doctrines, I believe, can be refuted.[1]

So the distinction between the transitive bodily sensations, which are bodily sense-impressions (feeling dry, feeling hot, feeling full), and the intransitive bodily sensations (aches, pains, itches, etc.), has not been explained. The fact that we cannot ask ourselves whether we *really* have a pain, an ache or an itch, at a certain place in our body remains an *unexplained* difficulty for the view that the intransitive

[1] Cf. *Perception and the Physical World*, chs. 3, 5 and 6.

bodily sensations are a species of bodily sense-impression.

But we have already seen that, if we try to assimilate the intransitive bodily sensations to any sensible qualities, it is natural to class them with the *secondary* qualities. Now somebody may reject a *complete* 'Phenomenalism of sensible qualities', may take a Realistic line about the primary qualities of objects, but may argue for a 'Phenomenalism of the *secondary* qualities.' It may be agreed that 'This is round' is not to be analysed in terms of the way things would look or feel to normal observers in standard conditions; but it may still be held that this is the correct analysis of 'This is blue', 'This is noisy', 'This is sour', 'This smells.' A vicious regress will be avoided, because an account of the qualities of normal observers, and standard conditions, can be given in terms of the *primary* qualities. When something looks blue to me, it really will be blue if my sense-impression corresponds to that of a normal observer in standard conditions. But when my hand feels itchy to me, there is no question of my feeling corresponding to physical reality, because, as a matter of contingent fact, there is only one observer to whom the hand yields 'itch-impressions'. Aches, pains, itches, tickles, etc., are a sort of proto-sense-impressions of proto-secondary qualities.

The truth or falsity of this account of the intransitive bodily sensations clearly depends on the truth or falsity of the doctrine of 'Phenomenalism of the secondary qualities'. And there are serious objections to this doctrine.

For this doctrine raises serious difficulties about the *unobserved* secondary qualities of objects. It seems perfectly intelligible to say that the walls of a deserted room are blue, that the room is warm, that the radio in the roon is making a noise, that there is a smell in the room, or there is a lump of sugar with a sweet taste in the room. Yet nobody is having any such sense-impressions.

It will be replied to this, of course, that in talking about the unobserved secondary qualities of objects we are simply talking about the *potential* sense-impressions of normal observers. But the trouble with this is that unseen colours, unfelt warmth, unheard sounds, unsmelt smells, untasted tastes, seem to be something much more than mere potencies. *Prima facie*, unperceived secondary qualities are just the same sort of thing as perceived secondary qualities. (There seems to be a world of difference between an unperceived secondary quality and an unfelt pain, itch or tickle.)

It may be objected to this that no unobserved sensible quality can be conceived except as a mere possibility of perception. But this is to relapse into a *complete* 'Phenomenalism of sensible qualities'. The theory we are examining purports to *distinguish* between, say, 'This is round, but nobody is looking at it or feeling it', and 'This is blue, but nobody is looking at it.' According to the theory, the first statement is not to be analysed solely in terms of the sense-impressions of potential observers, but the second statement must be so analysed. And the difficulty for a 'Phenomenalism of *secondary* qualities' is that there seem to be no grounds for such a sharp distinction.

It may be replied that modern physics shows us that there is no place for the secondary qualities in physical reality. But even if this were granted, for the sake of argument, it would surely have to be granted that it is only an *empirical discovery* that such qualities are not predicable of physical objects. If this is so, it would, *ipso facto*, make sense to predicate them of physical objects. We could *conceive* of physical objects that were coloured, whether perceived or unperceived. A 'Phenomenalism of the secondary qualities' might be true *de facto*, but not of logical necessity. But even if people felt pains, itches, tickles, etc., in numerically the same piece of flesh; talk about *unfelt* pains, itches and tickles would, of logical necessity, demand an account in terms of *potential* feeling of sensations at a place. 'There is a pain there, but nobody is feeling it', could not *conceivably* be parallel to 'This object is square, but nobody is looking at it or feeling it.' So a gap would remain between the secondary qualities and the intransitive bodily sensations.

A more plausible attempt to drive a *logical* wedge between the primary and the secondary qualities is to point to the different ways we check claims about such qualities. If a claim about a primary quality of an object is called in question, the ultimate court of appeal is *measurement*. But if a claim about the colour or taste of an object, or about a sound or a smell, is called in question, the ultimate court of appeal is to the way it appears to the majority under standard conditions. This difference in the method of checking claims, this difference in the method of verification, argues a difference in nature. And measurement is an objective technique, reliance on the normal perceiver a subjective one.

But I am not convinced that there is a real logical difference here. It is true that we usually employ very rough-and-ready techniques for deciding disputed questions about the secondary qualities. But we could use much more precise methods; for instance, in the case of colours we could use a colour chart. This seems to be like discovering lengths by measurement, instead of just 'judging by eye'. It may be objected here that use of a colour chart itself involves 'judging by eye', judging that the surface whose colour is to be identified is indistinguishable in colour from a certain coloured surface on the chart. But, of course, measurement of the primary qualities of objects *also* involves 'judging by eye', judging that two lines coincide, say.

It seems, therefore, that not only must we reject a 'Phenomenalism of the sensible qualities' but we must also reject a 'Phenomenalism of the secondary qualities'. So it still remains an objection to the attempt to identify the intransitive bodily sensations with bodily sense-impressions that the intransitive sensations do not correspond, or fail to correspond, to physical qualities.

## (ii) *Bodily sensations have a physical location*

It seems to make no sense to give sense-impressions a physical location. So in order to treat the intransitive bodily sensations as a species of bodily sense-impression, we were forced to translate statements like 'I have a pain in my hand' as 'I have a pain in the hand-part of my body-image.' Now this may seem a

71

very unsatisfactory translation, because the original statement appears to refer quite clearly to my *physical* hand, and not simply to a portion of the body-image.

But perhaps we should ask first whether it is really true that it makes no sense to talk of the physical location of sense-impressions. Consider the following cases. (*a*) I have a bitter taste in my mouth. It is shown to me conclusively that there is no real bitter taste in my mouth. I still say: 'Nevertheless, I have got a bitter taste in my mouth.' In this remark, 'bitter taste' clearly means a taste-*impression*. Yet I still locate the taste in a physical object, my mouth. (*b*) I say my hand feels hot. It is shown to me conclusively that my hand is not hot. I still say: 'Nevertheless, I have a feeling of heat in my hand.' Once again, we seem to have a sense-impression located in a physical object.

Despite these examples, however, it still seems very strange to talk of the physical location of sense-impressions. If there is an alternative way of taking these statements about the bitter taste and the feeling of heat it would obviously be preferable.

When I say that I have a bitter taste in my mouth in case (*a*), what is really meant, I think, is that I have a taste-impression *as of* a (real) bitter taste in my physical mouth. It is perceptually *as if* there were a bitter taste in my mouth. It is this putative real taste that I locate in my mouth, not my taste-impression. The same thing holds in case (*b*). When I say I have a feeling of heat in my hand, then I have a bodily sense-impression *as of* my hand being actually hot: it is perceptually *as if* I had a hot hand. It is the putative heat, a putative physical quality of the hand, that I locate in the hand, and not my thermal sense-impression.

This analysis enables us to understand what it is to 'locate' my visual sense-impression in my visual field, or my bodily sense-impression in my body-image. 'My visual field at a certain time' is simply my visual impressions *as of* certain real surfaces spatially related in a certain way. The 'spatial' relations of my visual impressions are simply the relations of these putative objects. In the same way, my body-image at a certain time is my bodily impressions *as of* certain events going on in the parts of my body. The 'spatial' relations of my bodily impressions are simply the spatial relations of these putative events.

But now it may be said that what is sauce for the goose is sauce for the gander. If we can translate 'I have a feeling of heat in my hand' as 'I have a feeling of heat in the hand-part of my body-image'; and if we can translate the second statement as 'I have a feeling *as of* physical heat in the hand of my physical body', why cannot we do the same for the intransitive bodily sensations? Let us translate 'I have a pain in my hand' as 'I have a pain in the hand-part of my body-image'; but then translate this second statement as 'I have a feeling *as of* pain in my physical body'.

But once the suggestion is made, we can see it will not do. For, unlike heat, we cannot have feelings *as of* pain, because there is no distinction between real and apparent pain. The suggestion, in fact, founders on the same rock that constituted the *first* objection to the reduction of intransitive bodily sensations to a species of bodily sense-impression. Intransitive bodily sensations do not reflect or fail to reflect physical reality: there are no pain- or itch-qualities to correspond to pain- or itch-impressions.

So, if we take the intransitive sensations as bodily sense-impressions, we must either shoulder the intolerable paradox of locating sense-impressions in our physical body; or else say that statements like 'I have a pain in my hand' mean 'I have a pain-impression in the hand-part of my body-image'; and refuse to translate this statement in the way we *can* translate statements about the 'location' of ordinary bodily sense-impressions. The second alternative is little happier than the first.

For the present, then, we have found two (interconnected) difficulties in saying that the intransitive bodily sensations are a species of bodily sense-impression. In fact I believe that these difficulties can be overcome, and that the intransitive sensations *are* a species of bodily impression. But for the present I want to beat around some neighbouring bushes. In the next four chapters I shall examine three other theories of the nature of the intransitive sensations. We shall then be in a position to develop a sounder view.

# CHAPTER ELEVEN

## INTRANSITIVE SENSATIONS AS LOCATED ITEMS

THE apparent failure of the suggestions that the intransitive bodily sensations are a species of sensible quality, or a species of sense-impression, leads on to the view that they are irreducibly themselves.

Perhaps we should say that they are simply unique and irreducible non-physical events, or, putting it in the most neutral way possible, non-physical *items*. (The view that they are *physical* events or items I take to be refuted by the arguments of Chapter 9.) They are items about whose nature we cannot be *radically* mistaken. They are items that cannot exist unfelt, and cannot have unfelt features, at any rate in anything but an attenuated sense. But they are not to be assimilated to anything else, they are *sui generis*, of their own sort.

This view may be held in two forms. In the first place, it may be said that these items are *located* in our body. In the second place, it may be held that these items are not locatable *in themselves*, and that we have to give some further account of their apparent location. In this chapter we shall discuss difficulties for the first view, in the next chapter we deal with the second view.

I shall offer four criticisms of the first view.

(i) The notion that a physical substance can have a non-physical quality, or be the place where a non-physical event or item can be located, seems to be a very curious one. At the very least, the notion stands in need of elucidation. It is not obvious that a physical substance can have non-physical predicates, or that a non-physical item can have a physical location.

(ii) We might reinforce this first argument in the following way. As we have noted, amputees report bodily sensations in places where their limb would be if they still had that limb. Now in what physical object are the amputees' sensations located, or what physical object do they qualify? The only available subject for the non-physical item or quality may be the vacant air. Yet surely we do not want to say that these items can float around in such a fashion?

The only way to escape this conclusion would be to say that in such cases we are radically mistaken about the real location of the sensation. But if this line is taken, it will presumably have to be said that there is *always* the logical possibility of a radical mistake in the location of *any* sensation. But although we have seen that there are some pressures in our thought and speech that push us in such a direction, the main drift of thought and speech is towards saying that the place of a bodily sensation is the place where it feels to be.

(iii) Another difficulty is created by the fact that, as

we have seen, the *esse* of bodily sensations is *sentiri*, that they cannot exist except where felt. It is true that we did allow sense to the phrase 'unfelt sensation', because we allowed the possibility of being *distracted* from our sensations. But it was suggested that the notion of an unfelt sensation should be analysed in terms of the sensations that we would *feel* if undistracted. If this is correct, the 'exception' really does prove the rule.

Now if the *esse* of bodily sensations is *sentiri*, there is a logical entailment holding between (i) the existence of a bodily sensation, and (ii) the existence of a mind which feels it. Now the hypothesis we are examining is that the bodily sensation is something actually located in, or qualifying, a portion of my body. If I have a pain in my hand, the pain is something non-physical that is somehow located in, or somehow qualifies, my hand. Now my hand, with its qualities, can exist in independence of a sentient subject; for instance, if cut off. We may grant Aristotle the linguistic point that it is not then to be called a 'hand' in the full sense; but this only means that included in the meaning of the word 'hand' is the relational predicate 'attached to a body'. But it is at least logically possible that the hand should have the same *intrinsic* properties that it had when attached to the body. (We might arrange to have blood circulate through it, etc.) Now if this is so, and if a bodily sensation is located in, or qualifies, my hand, why could not bodily sensations exist in my hand after it had been cut off, or when I am unconscious or dead? Why cannot the hand have *these* intrinsic properties like any other? And if we say that this is nonsense, as it seems to be, then this is a *reductio ad absurdum* of the view that bodily sensations are items located in, or qualities qualifying, my hand. The hypothesis is incompatible with the fact that sensations can exist only where there is a mind to feel them.

One answer to this argument would be to argue that there can be logically necessary connections between distinct things. The item in my hand, though distinct from my mind, is logically dependent upon it for its existence. To accept such a doctrine is to reject Empiricism. I cannot argue for the Empiricist principle here, I can only say that I accept it. The only alternative would be to deny that bodily sensations really were *intrinsic* features of parts of the body. But if not intrinsic features, they are relational features, and to make them relational features is surely to reject the hypothesis we are investigating. (And to say 'Here the distinction between intrinsic and relational features breaks down' is just to say 'I cannot answer the argument, but I am going to go on *saying* that bodily sensations are items located in my body, without bothering about any paradoxes I am led into.')

Of course, the three arguments we have advanced here depend on the assumption that the sensation-items are *physically* located. If 'I have a pain in my hand' means 'I have a pain in the hand-part of my body-image' then these arguments lose force. But, as we have seen, to talk about our body-image is only a fancy way of talking about bodily sense-impressions. Now the hypothesis at present under investigation is that the intransitive bodily sensations are unique in nature, and not to be identified with sense-impressions.

So if they are not located in our body there seems to be nowhere else to locate them.

(iv) My final argument holds against any account of the intransitive sensations as irreducible items, whether they are intrinsically located or not. The notion of an item about whose properties we cannot be mistaken is obviously a very difficult one. As Wittgenstein argues in the *Philosophical Investigations*, if one cannot be wrong about something, then one cannot be right about it either. The argument, I take it, is that if a mistake is logically impossible in a certain context, on a particular occasion, then there is no possibility of a contrast between being mistaken and not being mistaken. And when we rule out nothing, we say nothing.

It hardly mitigates the impact of this argument that we have conceded the possibility of the existence of a *limited* place for error about our current sensations. For then any statement about our current sensations that respected this margin of error would rule out nothing.

Of course, if Wittgenstein's argument is valid, it will not only apply to our intransitive bodily sensations, but also to all other current subjective experiences—to sense-impressions, mental images, thoughts, emotions, etc. But I am inclined to say that it *does* apply to all subjective experiences, and that the fact that we cannot be mistaken about them supplies us with an argument against treating such subjective experiences as any sort of object or item. (Unless we empty the words 'object' or 'item' of any force at all.) For example we can talk about 'sense-impressions', but we must not assume that even an attenuated substance corresponds to this substantive. It is quite beyond the scope of this book to argue the point here, but I would say that my sense-impressions are no more *objects* than are my impressions of life in Iceland in the days of the Sagas.

But the view of bodily sensations that we are considering explicitly takes them to be 'private objects' or 'private items', and in so doing it is forced to assume that talking about our current bodily sensations is reporting on current private items. And so it must face the criticism that if these reports are incorrigible we can give no force to the notion of a report.

It is true, of course, that it is very difficult to give any *alternative* account of 'first-person reports of present experience' which will do justice to their apparent incorrigibility, yet avoid the assumption that they are reports on 'private items'. And until a plausible alternative account is given, one may remain suspicious of Wittgenstein's argument here. But, at any rate, it is important to notice that the account of the nature of bodily sensations that we have been examining is particularly vulnerable to the Wittgensteinian line of argument against 'private items'.

# CHAPTER TWELVE

# INTRANSITIVE SENSATIONS AS UNLOCATED ITEMS

UNDER the influence of the first three arguments presented in the last chapter, one may be inclined to say that intransitive bodily sensations are *not* literally located in our body. In their own nature they are not in space, just as sense-impressions are not in space.

The great problem for such a view (besides that of answering the final objection of the last chapter) is to explain what we mean when we *speak* about the location of sensations. Can any satisfactory explanation of ordinary idiom be found? One answer readily suggests itself: an answer in terms of the physical *causation* of the sensation.

(i) *Is the 'place of the sensation' the place of the cause of the sensation?*

So let us now consider the suggestion that saying there is a certain sensation in a part of my body means that some physical event has occurred in part of my body, which causes me to have that sort of sensation. The word 'cause' here is meant to have all the imprecision of our ordinary use of the word, but it must be qualified by restriction to a *bodily* cause, to a happening in my *body* that causes me to have a sensation. (We know now that the only bodily happenings that give rise to bodily sensations are disturbances of certain nerve endings, or of the nerves themselves, or of certain portions of the brain. But since a phrase like 'I have a pain in my hand' was understood before these facts were known, they should not enter our analysis.)

Now there is no doubt that there is a close connection between the place of a pain (say), and the place of the bodily cause of the pain. I feel a pain in my hand, and on looking or touching I find a splinter embedded *where I feel the pain*. Normally, at any rate, the place of the pain *coincides* with the place of the bodily cause; the place where I feel the pain is the place which gives me pain when it is probed. Indeed, I think it is true to say that our ordinary concept of the place of pain *presupposes* the existence of this coincidence in the vast majority of cases. (In Chapter 15, when we advance our own theory of the nature of the intransitive sensations, we shall understand why this must be so.)

It is the coincidence between the place of pain and place of the cause of the pain that gives physical pain its great biological value. Since pain is something I want to stop, and since it is a biological fact that it usually occurs only when my body is suffering physical damage, if I am instinctively led to the place where the damage is being done I shall often be able to minimize the damage, thus promoting my chances of survival. (People who lack any feeling of pain in a certain limb regularly suffer serious injury to that limb in daily life.) Similar points could be made about most of the other intransitive sensations.

But the translation of 'I have a pain in my hand' into 'I have a pain whose bodily cause is in my hand' is unacceptable because a causal statement has a *hypothetical* character. It is at least logically possible for me to be *completely* wrong about the attribution of a cause. Now, as we have seen in Chapter 9, we are inclined to say that there can be only *marginal* error in the attributing of places to bodily sensations. It is true that we did call attention to a *tendency* in our thinking to allow the possibility of radical mislocation of bodily sensations. We noticed the case of the dentist who tells us that the pain is not in the jaw it feels to be in, or the doctor who says the sensations felt by an amputee are really in the stump. But this tendency co-exists with, is indeed very much overshadowed by, the tendency to say that the place of a bodily sensation must be pretty much where it feels to be. This is inexplicable if 'the place of the sensation' is *simply* the place of the bodily cause of the sensation. If this were correct, we should make no difficulty at all about admitting the possibility of being completely wrong about the place where the sensation is.

There is, however, one special case where 'the place of the pain' may seem to mean nothing but 'the place of the bodily cause of the pain'. Suppose I assign my pain an indeterminate location. That is to say, suppose I feel a pain in a certain area of my body, but do not feel the area to be painful *all over*, yet cannot locate the pain more precisely within the area. ('It's somewhere there, doctor.') In such a case we may resort to probing to fix the exact spot. Now the probing might make the pain *feel* to be located where the probe is. In that case, the *felt* location becomes more determinate.

But suppose this does not happen. Suppose that the felt location remains indeterminate, but pain is produced only when the probe is at a certain spot. We might still say that the probing had fixed the exact place of the pain. Yet here 'the exact place of the pain' seems to be nothing more than the place of the bodily cause of pain.

Notice, however, that even in such a case we would accept the result given by probing as the place of the pain only if this place falls *inside* the area where the pain originally felt to be. If the probe only caused pain in a *different* place, we should not be so happy about calling this place 'the place of the pain'. So even here an analysis in terms of the place of the bodily cause of pain is not complete.

(ii) *Is the 'place of the sensation' the place where we believe the cause of the sensation to be?*

But perhaps we can deal with this difficulty quite simply. Let us now say that the place of a sensation is not the place of the bodily cause of the sensation, but is rather the place where *we believe* the bodily cause of the sensation to be. A statement that our present belief is such-and-such is incorrigible, or more-or-less incorrigible, in just the same way that the attribution of places to bodily sensations is incorrigible, or more-or-less incorrigible. So if 'I have a pain in my hand' means 'I believe that the bodily cause of my pain is in my hand', the objection that causal statements are corrigible no longer applies.

Nor need we *completely* reject the original view that the place of the sensation is simply the place of the cause of the sensation. In ordinary language, it may be said, we take the place of the sensation to be *primarily* the place where we believe the bodily cause of the sensation to be. But this may be accompanied by some tendency to take the place of the sensation to be *simply* the place of the cause of the sensation. This may account for our understanding of the doctor or dentist when they say the pain is not really where it feels to be. We resist such remarks, *yet do not resist them altogether*.

But the new formula is still not satisfactory. Suppose I feel a pain in the upper jaw, but the dentist tells me that the *cause* of the pain is in the lower jaw, and I believe him. I still want to say that the pain feels to be in the upper jaw, and so *that is its location*. Yet I believe the cause to be in the lower jaw.

(iii) *Is the 'place of the sensation' the place where we believe, or are inclined to believe, the cause of the sensation to be?*

However, I think this objection can be met by a further modification of the formula. Perhaps we can say, in the case just described, that the thought is still with me that the cause of the pain is in the upper jaw. I do not account this thought true, because I believe the dentist, but the thought may remain with me all the same and even press towards being accepted as a belief. (Compare some cases of obsession. I may know very well that I have turned off the tap, yet the thought that I have not turned it off may remain with me and may even influence my actions.) Such a thought, pressing towards belief, but held back by

85

other knowledge, may be called an *inclination to believe*. So our new translation of 'I have a pain in my hand' will be 'I believe, or am inclined to believe, that the bodily cause of my pain is in my hand.'

But there still remain two objections to our twice-amended formula. One of the objections is not conclusive, but I think the other is.

## 1. HOW DO WE DISCOVER THE 'PLACE OF THE SENSATION'?

According to the view we are investigating, the *sensation itself* is not located, it is simply the putative bodily cause that is located. The question therefore arises how correlations are made between the sensation and 'the place of the sensation'. Clearly they will have to be discovered very early in life, because quite young children can point to the place where it hurts or itches.

It may seem that we must imagine the matter in some such way as this: the baby feels a pain (say), it then discovers, by touch or sight, that there is something unusual in contact with its skin. It removes the object or itself, and the pain goes. The next time it has a pain of the same qualitative sort, it takes the same action. Success in stopping the pain still further reinforces the association between pain and a particular place. (If this is not thought enough, we could postulate an innate tendency to believe that a particular sort of pain is caused by something happening at a particular place.) In this way, we come to know where the bodily causes of our sensations are, and we associate the places so closely with the sensation that we call such places 'the place of the sensation'. Very occasionally, we have the sort of sensation associated with one place, but it turns out that the cause of the sensation is elsewhere. But even when we know the cause is elsewhere, old habit is strong. We are still *inclined to believe* that the bodily cause of the sensation is at the old place, that is to say, *we feel the sensation there.*

Now the difficulty about this account is that it presupposes that there must be a qualitatively different sort of pain, itch, tickle, etc., for each different sensitive portion of the body. I feel a sudden pain, and I clap my hand to my left ear. Why do I think that the bodily cause of my pain is in the left ear rather than the right, or, for that matter, anywhere else in my body? I can do this only, it seems, if the pains associated with different bodily locations are qualitatively different sorts of pains. But is this in fact so? If I have a pain in my left ear, may it not be exactly the same sort of pain as a pain in my right ear? May it not be that the only difference between the pains is *the place where they are*? But since, on the view we are investigating, that place is only the place where we think the bodily cause to be, how could we associate the pain with one place rather than another? The present theory cannot explain this, except by the *ad hoc* device of postulating a different sort of pain for every different portion of the body. And the same line would have to be taken with every sort of intransitive bodily sensation that can be located in more than one place in the body.

However, Professor J. J. C. Smart has pointed out to me that this criticism depends upon taking too phenomenological an attitude to the problem of locating the bodily causes of our sensations. Suppose that there are differences in what happens *in the brain* as a result of the stimulation of pain-nerves in different parts of the body. As a causal result of the different happenings in the brain, we may just *find ourselves* with a belief, or inclination to believe, that the bodily cause of our pain is in a certain portion of our body; a belief or inclination to believe that is generally, although not always, correct. Such a belief would be *epistemologically immediate*: it would not rest upon any further knowledge, such as the knowledge that stimulation of certain parts of the body normally caused certain sorts of pain. At the same time, it would be *causally mediate*, for the belief or thought would come into our minds only as a result of a stimulation of the brain, normally occurring only when certain nerve-endings are stimulated in the part of the body where the pain is 'located'.

So there is no insuperable problem for this causal theory of the location of bodily sensations in explaining how we come to locate the place of the supposed cause of the sensation.

## 2. CAN THE 'PLACE OF THE SENSATION' BE NOTHING BUT THE PLACE OF THE SUPPOSED CAUSE?

But there is a simple objection to the view that 'I have a pain in my hand' means 'I believe, or am inclined to believe, that the bodily cause of the pain is in my hand.' It seems extraordinary to say that, when I talk of the place of a bodily sensation in ordinary speech, I am really talking about something quite different: *viz.* the place where I take, or am inclined to take, the *cause* of the sensation to be. Sensation and the cause of sensation must be two distinct things, and it would be an inexplicable idiom that talks of the supposed place of the cause of a thing as if it were the place of the thing itself.

I do not see that this simple objection can be met, and so I reject the whole attempt to analyse the location of intransitive bodily sensations in terms of the location of their causes.

The view that location is not part of the intrinsic nature of the intransitive bodily sensations must therefore give some other account of the locations that ordinary language appears to ascribe to such sensations. There is another account that may be suggested —the attitude-theory of the intransitive sensations— but we shall have to postpone a discussion of it until Chapter 14. In the meanwhile, we need only note that, unless some account can be given of ordinary idiom, the view that the intransitive bodily sensations are not intrinsically located must be abandoned.

---

# CHAPTER THIRTEEN

# ATTITUDES INVOLVED IN THE HAVING OF INTRANSITIVE SENSATIONS

BEFORE making yet another attempt to explain the nature of the intransitive bodily sensations, let us look at a feature of such sensations that we have hitherto ignored. It is part of what is involved in the having of most, if not all, intransitive bodily sensations that we take up certain attitudes to them, in particular, that we are sorry or glad to have them. Let us therefore run through some of the chief sorts of intransitive sensation, in order to see exactly what attitudes are involved. It will not be necessary, for our present purposes, to examine them all. We may begin with pains, including aches under the heading of 'pains'.

Our pain is something we would like to have stop. We consider it a bad thing, we have a con-attitude to it. A violent pain is a pain that we have an intense desire to have stop. We consider it a very bad thing, we have a very strong con-attitude to it. A mild pain we would rather like to have stop. We consider it a somewhat bad thing, we have a weaker con-attitude to it.

It is true that we may *endure* pain, some even

enduring it quite gladly, for the sake of something else. But this does not imply that we have a favourable attitude to the pain itself. However, the case of the masochist, and also the type of neurotic who 'seeks punishment', may be raised here. Do not they have a favourable attitude to pain itself?

But in fact this does not seem to be so. Consider the masochist first. It is not the case that 'his pain is his pleasure'. Taken literally, this implies that he has a favourable attitude to the thing he has an unfavourable attitude to, which is contradictory. What happens, I think, is that he finds certain features of some situations so pleasurable that he willingly puts up with pain for the sake of that pleasure. If this is correct, then we all act like masochists when we deliberately swallow scalding hot tea in order to warm ourselves up, or get into what is initially a painfully hot bath. All these things involve a good deal of 'hedonic sophistication': we have to *brace* ourselves to some degree to do these things for the ultimate pleasure they bring. (Consider our reaction when we swallow scalding tea, or get into a very hot bath, *unexpectedly*. I take it that the masochist who is hurt unexpectedly dislikes it is as much as the next man.)

The neurotic who 'seeks punishment', or who is said to 'seek punishment unconsciously', is a somewhat different case. For him, I think, the pain is endured, perhaps gladly endured, because it represents *expiation*. The pain is a punishment which assuages guilt. But the whole point about its being *punishment* is that it is something he has an unfavourable attitude to *in itself*. In itself it is something that he would rather be without; but it is better than unpunished guilt.

It is, then, a mark of physical pain that we do not like it for itself. We have an immediate desire that it should stop; we think of it as bad as an end, bad for its own sake, and not simply bad as a means.

Consider the case where serious damage is being done to our anaesthetized leg (and not for some good reason). We would undoubtedly want this to stop, we would think it a bad thing. But would we think it bad for its own sake, would we have an *immediate* desire that it should stop? I do not think so. The situation would be disliked, chiefly at least, for the things it brings on: bleeding, maiming, death. For if we felt no pain, and if we knew that afterwards the leg would renew itself like Prometheus' liver, most of our objections to the proceeding would be gone. This is the case with many bodily injuries that cause us no pain. If the injury produced different, and pleasanter, results from those it actually does produce, we would not call it an *injury*. But it is of the *essence* of pain that we wish it to stop.

It is a further mark of physical pain that our desire that it should stop is an *interested* as opposed to a *disinterested* desire. This is to be contrasted with aesthetic displeasure. Suppose I find a certain object aesthetically displeasing. This implies that if there is another object that is similar in all relevant respects, I will also find that object aesthetically displeasing. (Of course, I may dislike it only *in a certain setting*. But then the real object of aesthetic displeasure is 'the object in a certain setting', and the same remarks as before will apply to this new complex object.) If I find the object displeasing when my enemy owns it, but pleasing when I own it, then that is at least *prima facie* evidence that my emotions towards the object are not aesthetic ones. Aesthetic displeasure is thus, in a certain sense, impersonal or disinterested. But our dislike of physical pain is not in any way impersonal or disinterested. We want *our* pain to stop. A sadist may want *his* pain to stop, but have an immediate desire for *your* pain to continue.

So it is of the essence of physical pain that we have an *immediate* and *interested* desire that it should stop. Of course, pain is not the only thing for which we have this immediate and interested desire that it should stop. (Consider smelling an unpleasant smell: this is not physically *painful*.) But it is a fact about human beings that, in normal circumstances, their dislike of physical pain is stronger than anything else.

It seems, furthermore, that in physical pain we have a special attitude to the place where the pain is located. Freud remarks:

When there is physical pain a high degree of what may be called narcissistic cathexis of the painful place occurs.[1]

This seems to be a conceptual remark. When we have a pain in our hand, we are *concerned* about our hand, with a concern that is immediate and interested. Our hand absorbs our attention. This concern for our hand is a *loving* concern: we are annoyed by the pain, but we are not annoyed by our hand. We dislike the pain, but we do not dislike the place 'where the pain is'. On the contrary, that is a place which, as children say, we want 'kissed and made better'. Hating the sin, we love the sinner.

[1] *Inhibitions, Symptoms and Anxiety*, translated by Alix Strachey, p. 170.

This loving concern with the painful place may be contrasted with the emotion of *disgust* that we may feel for some thing or happening, including things or happenings in our own body. There is no loving concern for the object of disgust; we hate both the sin and the sinner.

So physical pain, in its typical manifestations at least, involves an immediate and interested desire that it should stop, and a loving concern for the painful place. It will be helpful to have a brief phrase to cover this whole complex of attitudes towards pain. Let us call it 'the pain-reaction'. Of course we must not let this name deceive us into assuming without argument that it is *only* to physical pains that we have the pain-reaction. But physical pains do call forth this reaction: it is part of their essence that they should do so.

The attitudes involved in having an *itch* are simply described. We have an immediate and interested dislike of our itches, just as in the case of pain. Our dislike of our itches is, however, not as extreme as our dislike of our pains. It is true that some itches can be worse than some pains. It is true, also, that we do speak of 'unbearable itches'. But if we had a choice between an 'unbearable itch' and an 'unbearable pain' it is clear which we would choose.

Our attitude to the itchy place is also simply described. We want to alleviate the itch by scratching or rubbing the spot, or doing something similar.

*Tickles* are not sharply cut off from itches. In general, we have an immediate and interested dislike of them. So far as they are distinguished from itches, they seem to involve tactual perception: perception of a light contact between our skin and something

94

moving over it. It is characteristic of a tickle that we seek to break this contact by withdrawing from the tickling thing.

But not only do tickles merge into itches, they also merge into erotic sensations. People tickle each other for pleasure. However there always seems to be an ambivalent attitude involved. Even if we like being tickled, we still have a tendency to withdraw from the tickling object.

*Erotic sensations* are normally pleasurable; we have an immediate and interested liking for them, But we *may* dislike them, or be indifferent to them.

*Tingles* seem to be a perfectly neutral sort of sensation. We may dislike having, like having, or be indifferent to having, tingles.

# CHAPTER FOURTEEN

# INTRANSITIVE SENSATIONS AS ATTITUDES

HITHERTO we have assumed that, whatever the intransitive bodily sensations are, they are the objects of some sort of cognitive process. To have a bodily sensation is to perceive a quality of the body, or it is to have a bodily sense-impression, or it is to apprehend a unique non-physical item located in the body, or it is to apprehend an item that is not located in the body yet is somehow associated with parts of the body. But, it may be argued, this assumption is the root of the trouble. In the previous chapter we have seen the extent to which certain attitudes are built into our concepts of bodily sensations. Perhaps, then, to have a certain sort of bodily sensation is simply *to take up a certain attitude towards a portion of the body.*

Such a theory is most simply worked out in the case of *itches*. It is natural to think of an itch as something that is there in a certain place in our body. Being there (whatever 'being there' means), it evokes a desire to scratch or rub that spot. But perhaps we should think of the matter in a different way. Perhaps we should say that it is our desire to scratch or rub a certain spot that constitutes having an itch at that spot. It is easy to think that the order 'Point to the itch' is like the order 'Point to the ink bottle.' But perhaps it is really more like saying 'Point to the one you prefer.' The ink bottle exists independently of your pointing to it, but your choice may be *constituted* by the one to which you point. (This is not to say that such a choice must be *arbitrary*. Nor is it arbitrary when you point to the place where the itch is.) It may be noted that such an account of itches explains why we cannot make any major mistake about their nature and location.

So on this view an itch is nothing but a more or less violent immediate and interested desire (an *impulse*) to rub or scratch a certain spot. There could also be a weaker form of the theory. In Chapter 12 we examined the view that bodily sensations are mental items that are not *intrinsically* located. The difficulty for this view was to say what it meant to *ascribe* a location to such sensations. We examined, and rejected, an account of the 'location' of sensations in terms of the location of their supposed bodily cause. But now we have an alternative solution to the difficulty. While denying that an itch is simply an impulse to rub or scratch a certain spot, we could still say that the so-called 'place of the itch' was the place we were impelled to rub or scratch *when we had an itch*. (And we could do justice to the causal theory of location by saying that the place we were impelled to rub or scratch was normally the place of the cause of the itch.) Let us call this theory the attitude-theory of the *location* of intransitive sensations, in contradistinction to the attitude-theory of the intransitive sensations themselves.

An attitude-theory of tickles would say that having a tickle is just a matter of trying to break the contact between a portion of our skin and the 'tickling' object, or of having an impulse to rub the 'ticklish' spot. An attitude-theory of the *location* of tickles will say that 'the place of the tickle' is the place we are impelled to withdraw from contact with another object (which is causing the tickle), or the place we are impelled to rub.

How can we give an attitude-theory of aches and pains? We shall have to say that the 'narcissistic cathexis', which Freud speaks of as directed to the painful place, actually *constitutes* the pain. To have a pain in a certain place is just to be sorry for that place, to give that place attention, apply treatment to that place, and so on. On the attitude-theory of the *location* of pain we will say that these attitudes to a certain place give a sense to talking of the *location* of pains, without constituting the pain itself. And we could fill this view out by saying that normally the place towards which the 'narcissistic cathexis' is directed is the place of the *cause* of the pain, and the place where suitable procedures will alleviate the pain.

An attitude-theory of erotic sensations would have to run along the same lines as an attitude-theory of pain. Instead of an immediate and interested concern over the condition of a portion of our body, there is an immediate and interested pleasure. An attitude-theory of the *location* of erotic sensations would also run parallel to an attitude-theory of the location of pains.

Similar accounts might be given of the other intransitive sensations, or of their location.

But such attitude-theories face many serious difficulties.

(i) In the first place, what are we to say about such sensations as *tingles*? As we noted in the previous chapter, there seem to be no attitudes involved in any way in the concept of a tingle. We could not say that having a tingle is just being prepared to point to a certain spot! And even if we only wanted to give an attitude-theory of the *location* of tingles, it is a thin explanation to say that the place of a tingle is only the place we are prepared to point to (a place which is normally the place of the cause of the tingle).

(ii) But even if we forget about tingles, there remains a clear distinction between itches and tickles, on the one hand, and pain and erotic sensations, on the other. Where we have an itch or tickle our attitude can be clearly described. We want to rub or scratch the itching place, we want to withdraw or rub the tickling place. But it is much more difficult to describe the attitudes that are supposed to constitute the pain or the erotic sensation without falling into circularity. When I have a pain in my hand, the natural description of my attitude to my hand is that I want *the pain there to stop*. But this presupposes that having a pain in my hand is something independent of my attitude to my hand, which contradicts the hypothesis being investigated. Other attempts to describe the attitude seem thin and implausible. Mere solicitude for my hand ('narcissistic cathexis') could not amount to pain in the hand. The same sort of remarks apply, even more strongly, to erotic sensations. There seems to be no remotely convincing description of the attitude involved except to say that we take pleasure in having a certain sort of sensation at a certain place.

The same criticisms apply, perhaps less forcefully, if we simply put forward an attitude-theory of the *location* of pains and erotic sensations. Are we prepared to say that the place of the pain is simply the place for which we have an immediate and interested concern (a place which is normally the place of the cause of the sensation)? It does not seem to be enough. And what do we say about the 'place' of erotic sensations?

(iii) The two previous objections, it may be said, simply show the limited applicability of the attitude-theory (in either form). It still remains a perfectly satisfactory account of itches and tickles (or of the 'location' of itches and tickles). But the next difficulty to be mentioned affects itches and tickles too.

It is possible for intransitive bodily sensations (like the other bodily sensations) to be scarcely felt or to be very faint. Now such sensations, it seems, may be unaccompanied by any pro- or con-attitude to them, or to the place where they are located. A very faint itch or tickle or pain may not trouble us at all. It may arouse no attitude whatsoever. Yet we still have such sensations, and we give them a bodily location, just as in the case of bodily sensations that do move us.

(iv) The fourth difficulty is based on rather unusual cases, and it is difficult to know how to assess it. There are situations where people report that they have pains, but they say that the pain is not giving them any sort of concern.[1] If we are to take these reports at face value, it seems that physical pain does not always involve taking up some attitude to the pain, or to the 'place of the pain'.

(v) Finally, even if we waive all these objections, and even if we consider the most plausible cases, that is, itches and tickles, there is still an unsatisfactory feel about this analysis of the nature of the intransitive sensations or of their location. I think we are very loath to say that in pointing to the place of an itch we are simply pointing to the place we are impelled to rub or scratch. We have the strongest inclination to say that we want to rub or scratch that place because we feel *that something is going on there*. I do not think we can dismiss this inclination as mere metaphysical double-vision.

So although attitudes may play a part in explaining what it is to have a bodily sensation, or what it is to locate bodily sensations, we cannot accept the view that such attitudes exhaust the nature of the sensation, or exhaust the notion of 'the place of the sensation'. We must reject an attitude-theory of the intransitive sensations. Nor can an attitude-theory of location solve the problem of location for a theory that holds that the intransitive sensations are *intrinsically* unlocated.

[1] Cf. Wegner, Jones and Jones, *Physiological Psychology*, ch. 8, p. 107: 'Discussing prefrontal lobotomy for the relief of unbearable pain the authors say: 'When questioned after such an operation, the patient often admits that his pain is still there, but that it no longer bothers him; . . .'

# CHAPTER FIFTEEN

# INTRANSITIVE SENSATIONS AS SENSE-IMPRESSIONS (II)

**B**UT now let us return to the view that the intransitive bodily sensations are sense-impressions of our bodily state. We saw many resemblances between our sense-impressions and our intransitive bodily sensations. We also saw that what we called the *transitive* bodily sensations—sensations of warmth, pressure, motion, etc.—were simply bodily sense-impressions. But there remained two intertwined difficulties in this account of the intransitive bodily sensations. In the first place, it seemed that our intransitive bodily sensations do not, as sense-impressions do, correspond or fail to correspond to the physical state of affairs. If my hand feels to me to be hot, I can go on to ask whether or not the hand is hot in physical reality. But if my hand feels sore, I cannot go on to ask whether it is sore in physical reality. In the second place, we give our intransitive bodily sensations a bodily location, but it seems to make no sense to speak of the physical location of sense-impressions. It is true that we may say 'I have a feeling of heat in my hand', but this may be translated as 'I have a feeling *as of* my hand being (physically) hot.' But if we try to translate 'I have a feeling of pain in my hand' as 'I have a feeling *as of* my hand being (physically) sore', we are once again stopped by the absence of any distinction between felt pain and real pain.

Can we get over these difficulties? Consider the statement 'My vision became blurred.' Here we seem to have a statement about visual sense-impressions. Nevertheless, 'looking blurred' is quite different from 'looking blue'. If I put on blue spectacles, things will look blue. But it makes sense to ask 'Are things really blue or not?' If my eyes fill with tears, things will look blurred. But it makes no sense to ask 'Are things really blurred or not?' There is a distinction between real and apparent blueness, but no distinction between real and apparent blurredness.

Nevertheless, if things look blurred to me, we can still give a discription of the way things look in purely physical terms. For what we mean by saying things look blurred is that it looks *as if* the light has become dimmer, the outlines of things have begun to waver physically, the air has become mistier, etc. I do not claim that this translation is very accurate, for to talk about 'blurring' is to talk about something that is highly idiosyncratic, which is why we have a special word. But I do claim that it is at least logically possible for there to be physical changes in the environment which, if veridically perceived, would yield the same visual appearances as those obtained in 'blurring'. And the description of the physical changes would be something like the changes mentioned above. It is true, of course, that we use the word 'blurred' in such a way that it is implied that such physical changes have *not* taken place, that the change is simply in our visual impressions. But we can still describe the change in our visual impressions when our vision blurs, by saying that it is *as if* these physical changes had taken place.

Now, although there is no distinction between real and apparent blurriness, there is a distinction between real and apparent dimming of light, real and apparent waverings of outline, real and apparent misting. And we can replace talk about blurring by talk about apparent dimmings, waverings and mistings, although such replacements may fail to do justice to nuances.

This example may embolden us. Can we do the same in the case of the intransitive bodily sensations? Can we *translate* statements about such sensations, so that they become ordinary statements about certain bodily sense-impressions we are having, sense-impressions which will correspond or fail to correspond to physical reality?

Let us begin by considering the two sorts of intransitive bodily sensation to which we do not assign a bodily location, *viz.* giddiness and dizziness. (We allowed that dizziness was a 'conflict case', because there is some tendency to say that dizziness is in the head.) As with the intransitive bodily sensations that *are* located, we cannot make a distinction between real and apparent giddiness or dizziness.

To feel giddy normally involves the feeling of being on the verge of falling, or of losing one's balance. To the extent that it involves this, it is not a matter of having a bodily *sensation* at all, but of having what we previously called a *bodily feeling*, meaning by 'bodily feelings' such things as feeling fresh, feeling tired, feeling faint, etc. But giddiness does seem to involve bodily sensation also. How shall we describe that sensation? When we have that sensation, I think, we feel that our body as a whole and its environment are moving in relation to each other with the characteristic 'round-and-round' motion. I deliberately say that the sensation is a feeling that our body and its environment are moving in relation to each other, and not simply a feeling that our body is moving, because giddiness involves the characteristic tendency to 'project' the motion of the body on to the environment. We should notice also that the motion that feels to obtain in giddiness is a highly idiosyncratic one (which is part of the reason for the existence of the special *word* 'giddiness'). Hence to talk of the motion as a 'round-and-round' one is only to render its nature in a rough-and-ready manner. (Compare 'My vision is blurred.') But it seems that to feel giddy is simply to feel that our body and its environment are moving in certain relations to each other, together with the feeling of being on the verge of falling.

Now if this analysis of giddiness is correct, we can see that in so far as giddiness is a bodily sensation, it is simply a bodily sense-impression. For although there is no contrast between real and apparent giddiness, there *is* a contrast between real and apparent motions of the body in relation to the environment. So, although we cannot say 'I feel giddy, but am I really giddy?', we *can* say 'I feel giddy, but are my body and its environment really moving in relation to each other in the characteristic 'round-and-round' way?'

A similar account can be given of dizziness. Like giddiness, dizziness normally involves certain bodily *feelings*, in particular a tendency to feel faint. It also involves a dimming or blurring of our perceptions generally. But over and above this, I think, there is the feeling that our *head* is moving in relation to the rest of our body, and to the environment, in a certain sort of way. (It is the fact that dizziness has something to do with our head that gives some countenance to the 'location' of dizziness *in* the head.) The motion that feels to be going on is similar to, although not, I think, identical with, the motion that feels to be going on when we say our head is 'swimming'. If this is correct, to feel dizzy is, in part at least, to have a certain sort of bodily sense-impression. We can say 'I feel dizzy, but is my head really moving in relation to my body and the environment in a certain (highly idiosyncratic) way?'

Emboldened by these successes, let us now try to produce similar translations in the case of the *located* intransitive bodily sensations. We shall find the task rather more complicated, and not without some difficulties, but I think the same line of thought will apply as in the cases of giddiness and dizziness.

Let us begin by considering *pain*. To have a pain in a certain place, we now say, is to feel a disturbance of our normal bodily state at that place; together with an immediate and interested dislike of that feeling; and a concern for the place where the disturbance feels to be. What is the nature of the disturbance that is felt to be taking place? It may be felt as nothing but 'a disturbance'. We cannot say 'My hand feels sore, but is it really sore?'; but we could say 'It feels as if there is a disturbance going on in my hand (a bodily impression that arouses certain attitudes in me), but is there really any disturbance going on in my hand?' Physical pain becomes a certain sort of highly indeterminate bodily sense-impression, an impression which happens to arouse certain (quite determinate) attitudes in the person who has it.

There are difficulties for this hypothesis, but we shall reserve them for the next chapter. For the present, let us dwell on the explanatory power of this account of physical pain.

Having a certain sense-impression does not entail taking up any particular attitude to that impression. It is a contingent fact that we like or dislike certain bodily sense-impressions. But it is now being suggested that the concept of physical pain is a portmanteau-concept: that it involves *both* the having of a certain sort of bodily sense-impression, *and* the taking up of a certain attitude to the impression. The *painfulness* of the sense-impression is therefore a *relational* property of the impression, in just the same way that the pain-fulness of a scene is a relational property of that scene. We call physical pain 'pain' simply because the having of these impressions of bodily disturbance is normally the most painful thing in human life.

It will be noted that this portmanteau nature of the concept of physical pain means that the statement 'I have a pain in my hand' has a double incorrigibility. For it involves asserting that I am having a certain sense-impression, and asserting my dislike of having that impression.

Once we see that the concept of physical pain is a portmanteau concept, involving *both* impression and reaction to impression, the possibility at once arises that the bodily feeling could occur without the usual reaction. Now it might be suggested here that this is what happens in the case of the masochist. He feels something to be going on, but he rejoices in it. However, although it is a logical possibility that such a thing should take place, I very much doubt whether this is the situation of the *masochist*. As I have argued earlier, he is enduring pain for the sake of the accompanying pleasures (pleasures that may be as much conceptual as bodily).

But the possibility of separating impression and reaction may explain what is happening in those situations where people report 'pain', but also report that they are quite unworried by the pain. Perhaps we can construe such extraordinary reports as implying that they feel something take place in their body, a feeling which they recognize would ordinarily evoke the pain-reaction, but which is not doing so in this case. The reaction is abolished, but not the impression. In such an unusual situation, a linguistic decision has to be taken as to whether they can be said to be feeling 'pain' or not.

We may explain the very mild pain that elicits no reaction from us in the same way. In such a case, we may say, we still feel a bodily disturbance at a certain place, the *sort* of disturbance that does elicit a pain-reaction in us; but in this case what is happening is insufficient to elicit that reaction. (A difficulty that arises here will be considered in the next chapter.)

The case of the pain in the amputated limb is easily explained by this analysis of physical pain. To locate a pain in a portion of our body is to feel *as if* there were a disturbance in that portion of our body (and to have the characteristic 'pain-reaction' to that feeling). Such a bodily impression may correspond or fail to correspond to physical reality; there may or may not be a physical disturbance in that portion of the body. In the case of the amputated leg we have *bodily sensory illusion*, for there is no such disturbance in the place where there feels to be a disturbance. Indeed it is a peculiarly radical form of sensory illusion, which may be called an *hallucination* of bodily sense. (Cf. Chapter 6.) For not only are we under illusion in feeling there to be any actual disturbance in that place, we are also under illusion in feeling to have a leg at all. (In confirmation of this account of the pain in the amputated leg, it may be noticed that it is traditional for philosophers to mention it when they discuss sensory illusion.)

This enables us to understand why there is *some* pressure in our thinking to allow the possibility of a radical mislocation of our pains; a pressure to say that the amputee's pains are really in the stump, or the pain felt in the upper jaw is really in the lower jaw. What we are tempted to do in such cases is to substitute for the place where the disturbance feels to be occurring (which is normally what we mean by 'the place of the pain'), the place where the actual disturbance is. And it may be quite useful for doctors and others to speak of 'the real place of the pain', meaning by this the place of the disturbance that is actually giving us pain.

Now, also, we are in a position to see the true merits of the causal theory of the *location* of pains, discussed and rejected in Chapter 12. First, however, we must appreciate the role of the concept of causation in perception.[1] In veridical perception, we can say that the object perceived is the cause of the perception. Suppose

[1] A point emphasized by Dr. C. B. Martin, of Adelaide University, which I have learnt from him.

I have a veridical perception of an orange rolling into my field of view. We can say that this event (the orange rolling into view) caused my perception of the event. For if that event had not occurred, and everything had remained normal otherwise, I would have had no such perception. In sensory illusion, of course, the 'thing perceived' cannot be the cause of the illusory perception.

Now consider the statement 'My hand feels sore.' This is being translated as 'It feels as if there is a disturbance going on in my hand: a bodily impression that arouses certain attitudes in me.' Now suppose that this bodily impression corresponds to physical reality, that there really is such a disturbance going on in my hand. This would be a case of veridical perception. Now if it is a case of veridical perception, the thing perceived (the disturbance) should be the cause of the bodily impression. And, of course, this is the case. The disturbance in the hand brought about the impression of the disturbance. If the disturbance had not occurred, there would have been no bodily impression. So we can say that, in such a case, the 'place of the pain' is not only the place where something is, and feels to be, going on; but it is *also* the place of the cause of the bodily feeling. That is to say, it is the place of the cause of the pain. And in the case of the amputated leg the 'place of the pain' is not only the place where something feels to be going on, it is also the place which we (falsely) believe, or are inclined to believe, is the place of the cause. So to say 'the place of the pain' is the place of the putative cause of the pain is to bring out a necessary *part* of our concept of 'the place of the pain', although it is not the full story.

How does our analysis distinguish between aches and pains? In both cases, it seems, it feels to us as if a disturbance were occurring in a certain part of our body, and we have an immediate and interested dislike of that feeling, together with a solicitude for the place where the disturbance feels to be. Yet although aches may be described as a species of physical pain, not all physical pains are aches.

Let us recall some special features of aches. We associate an ache with a much larger area than other pains, yet, at the same time, the location of an ache is much less determinate. We can only vaguely indicate the affected area. Aches do not occur on the surface of our body, but only at some depth. They are associated especially with the muscles. It is natural to think of aches as having a *volume*, unlike many pains which seem to have only a two-dimensional location on the skin. Aches characteristically come into being, increase in intensity and die away, relatively slowly. At their worst, they are more endurable than the worst pains. These features, I suggest, *constitute* the aching quality of aches, and mark them off from other pains. Anything we call an ache has some (normally all) of these special characteristics. It is clear that these features can be quite easily dealt with by our method of translation.

Besides pains and aches I am inclined to recognize a third class which we might call *bodily discomforts*. Some bodily discomforts are readily describable in terms of *transitive* bodily sensations. For instance, the discomfort of pressure on the bladder often involves a sensation of pressure, together with an immediate and interested dislike of the sensation. But in some cases of

111

discomfort our bodily impression may be of nothing more than 'something-or-other going on in a certain place' or perhaps 'something amiss at a certain place.' How do we distinguish such discomforts from pains and aches? I think they are more like aches than pains, but are even more vaguely and indeterminately located than aches. They come into being and die away even more gradually, and, characteristically, are not so intense. There seems to be no sharp distinction between aches and bodily discomforts.

Further problems about pain we will postpone to the next chapter. We go on now to consider *itches*.

To have an itch in a certain place is to feel a disturbance of our normal bodily state at that place, together with an immediate and interested dislike of that feeling, and an impulse to try to remove the disturbance by rubbing or scratching. Even with a violent itch, the immediate and interested dislike is not as extreme a dislike as that involved in violent pain. But the thing that clearly differentiates an itch from, say, a prick is the presence of the impulse to rub or scratch. What about the case of a very mild itch, so mild that there is no such impulse? We answer that, just as in the case of very mild pain, the bodily impression is called an itch because we recognize that the impression belongs to the *class* which normally evokes an impulse to rub or scratch. (I will say something more about this in the next chapter.)

*Tickles* are a slightly more complex phenomenon. They seem to involve not merely bodily, but also tactual, perception. When we have a tickle we have (i) a feeling that our body is in light contact with an object that is moving over our body; (ii) a feeling that

112

there is a disturbance of our normal bodily state at the place of contact; (iii) an immediate and interested dislike of these feelings; (iv) an impulse to try to remove both feelings by breaking contact with the tickling object; (v) finally, if this action fails to remove the second or bodily feeling, an impulse to rub or scratch the part of the body that feels affected.

It may be noticed that the dislike mentioned in (iii) does not always occur. We may enjoy being tickled. But this enjoyment always seems to have some ambivalence of quality. The child enjoys being tickled, but tries to avoid being tickled at the same time. Notice also that the impulse to withdraw mentioned in (iv) may on occasion be so compelling as to be almost a reflex. Notice finally that if withdrawal has occurred but the tickle remains, the sensation seems to be then indistinguishable from a (mild) itch. It can only be differentiated *by its previous history.*

*Erotic sensations* are something different again. There is a sense in which one can say that there is no such class of sensations. (It is significant that there is no untechnical class name.) When we have erotic sensations I do not think that we are confined to a highly indeterminate impression that 'something-or-other is going on' in a region of our body. What we have is *various sorts* of bodily (and tactual) impressions, impressions of more or less specific bodily happenings and bodily contacts, impressions for which we have an immediate and interested liking. We might even say that erotic sensations are wrongly classified as intransitive sensations. They are, instead, certain transitive bodily sensations. (And we can, of course, take up other attitudes besides that of liking to such sensations.)

In fact I think that there is no clear distinction to be made between erotic sensations and other impressions of bodily happenings and contacts for which we have an immediate and interested liking. This, I think, is the conceptual basis of the Freudian extension[1] of the terms 'erotic sensations' to include pleasures not always put under this head: such things as the sensations involved in sucking, in excretion, etc. For there is no clear mark to distinguish impressions of such happenings from more specifically sexual sensations. In all such cases we have immediate and interested pleasure in bodily feelings. All we can say to mark off the erotic sensations is that there are certain bodily feelings and feelings of contact in which most human beings take the greatest pleasure. Any other such feelings that bring comparable pleasure tend to be called erotic sensations also. (But it is also a *social* matter what sensations are called erotic.)

*Nausea* should be classified as a bodily feeling in many cases, not a bodily sensation. It is the feeling of being on the verge of being sick, or, simply, it is feeling sick. But sometimes at any rate it seems to involve bodily sensation in the region of the stomach. In such cases what we have is a bodily discomfort, a feeling that something is going on in the general region of the stomach for which we have an immediate and interested dislike. It is the accompaniment of the bodily feeling of feeling sick that turns it into nausea.

*Hunger* is primarily the desire to eat. But the hunger-pangs that regularly accompany this desire are feelings that something is going on in our stomach. And

[1] I am not suggesting that the extension did not also have an empirical basis, or at least a presumed empirical basis.

114

although, uninstructed, we could give no very clear account of the matter, there is a perception of the difference between what goes on in the stomach when we feel sick, and what goes on when we feel hungry.

*Thirst* is the desire to drink. But it is often accompanied by sensations of dryness in the mouth and throat.

*Tingles* are a difficult class of intransitive bodily sensations to bring under our general scheme. A bit tentatively, I suggest the following translation. 'I feel a tingle in my ear' is to be rendered as 'It feels to me as if a multitude of small motions or disturbances were taking place in my ear.' Although there is no distinction between real and apparent tingles, there is a distinction between the real and apparent occurrence of such happenings. We need take up no particular attitude to our tingles. But perhaps 'pins and needles' could be described as a violent tingling for which we have an immediate and interested dislike.

Having now put forward our theory of the nature of intransitive bodily sensation, we shall finish this study by considering criticisms that might be brought against it. Answering the criticisms should further elucidate the theory. We shall concentrate particularly on the key case of *pain*.

# CHAPTER SIXTEEN

# OBJECTIONS ANSWERED

## 1. WHAT DO WE FEEL TO BE HAPPENING AT THE PLACE OF THE SENSATION?

It may seem impossible to introduce the notion of a feeling that something is going on in our body into our account of such sensations as pain. For *what* is it that we feel to be going on? On occasion we may be able to describe what feels to be going on in a rough-and-ready way ('it feels as if they are sticking something into me'). But on other occasions this is impossible. Faced with this difficulty, one is tempted to say that it is the *sensation* which we feel at the place. And this would make our analysis circular.

But what is the objection to saying that what feels to me to be going on in a certain part of my body is something quite unspecific? Why could we not have the feeling *that* something is going on, without being able to say *what* it is? We can normally say pretty definitely where the happening feels to be (we can indicate the place of the sensation); and our reaction to the feeling may be perfectly clear (in the case of pain, for instance, we do not want it); but what feels to be going on we may hardly be able to say. It is

just a feeling that something untoward is happening
there.

(In any case, however, I think we can say that the
nature of the felt happening must be the sort of thing
perceived by bodily sense or touch. That is, it must be
some motion or other spatial determination of our
body or some object in contact with our body, or else
a thermal property of the body or some object in
contact with the body.)

The following case, taken from sight, may help to
reconcile us to the situation. I may find that a certain
arrangement of visual objects arouses displeasure in
me. Yet I may be unable to say just what it is in the
arrangement that arouses my displeasure. Suppose,
then, that in my absence the arrangement is slightly
altered. On seeing it again, I am able to say (*a*) it has
been altered, (*b*) it is now pleasing. Yet I am quite unable to say what the beneficial alteration was, except
that it was a visual alteration. All this seems possible.
Here I saw a certain arrangement, and it aroused an
unfavourable reaction in me, yet I was unable to say
*what* it was that displeased. Later the changed arrangement pleased me, yet I was unable to say *what* the
beneficial change was.

In the same way (to take the case of pain), may I
not feel that something is going on in a portion of my
body, want to be rid of it, and yet be unable to say
anything more about what it is that feels to go on?
And later on, may it not feel that the displeasing
happening has stopped, although I still do not know
in any more detail what it was that stopped?

It is also helpful to remember here, once again,
what extremely imprecise information we gain by

bodily feeling. What we know straight-off about our body, through bodily feeling alone, is nothing very determinate. We can become aware that our temperature is up, our limbs are moving, our stomach or gut full, our heart thumping, our muscles tensed. But if we were asked to specify these happenings in any more detail, by means of bodily feeling alone, we should be stumped. Even the perceptions just mentioned incorporate a certain amount of information not gained originally by bodily sense. If we restricted ourselves to what is *immediately* perceived, the perceptions would be even more indeterminate.

When we think of sense-perception, we have a strong impulse to think of *sight*. Now our eyes yield us remarkably detailed and precise impressions of the world. But bodily perception is far less efficient. In the case of the intransitive sensations, perhaps, our bodily perception approaches the limit of imprecision except with respect to location.

But, in the important case of pain, at any rate, we may have been yielding too much ground to the objection. With bodily pain it is far from clear that our bodily feeling is always limited simply to 'something-or-other going on' at a certain location. For here we must recall the great variety of *descriptions* that we give our physical pains. For instance, we speak of throbbing, stabbing, stinging, pricking, searing, burning, racking, bursting or tearing pain.

Now, to some extent, these descriptions are descriptions of the *intensity* of the pain. A stabbing, stinging, searing, racking or tearing pain must be a fairly *severe* pain. A pricking pain is milder. And intensity, or severity, we have suggested, is to be analysed in terms of the strength of our dislike of having the feeling. All things being equal, a pricking pain is a lesser evil than a stinging pain. And a prickle is a lesser evil still.

In some cases, also, these descriptions of a pain are descriptions of its temporal pattern and temporal duration. A *throbbing* pain rapidly waxes and wanes in intensity. (Compare feeling a tic.) A *twinge* of pain is not only a mild pain, but it lasts a short time. A *flash* of pain also lasts a short time, although the pain itself is more severe.

But this is not all there is to these descriptions. If I say my pain is a throbbing one, am I not also saying that there feels to be some sort of *pulsation* in the part of the body where the pain is? If I speak of a stabbing, stinging or pricking pain am I not saying that it feels as if my flesh is being disturbed by some sharp-pointed thing like a blade or a sting or a pin? A racking pain seems to be a pain where my muscles feel as if they are being stretched. When I have a burning pain my body feels as if burning heat is being applied to it, internally or externally.

The bodily feelings involved may be vague in the extreme, and unreliable in the extreme, but they do seem to involve an awareness, however vague and unreliable, of the *nature* of what is going on in our body when we feel the pain as opposed to intensity, location, and temporal pattern. So it is not *always* true, at any rate, that when we feel pain all we feel is that 'something-or-other is going on' in a certain place.

It may be objected here that 'a stabbing pain' (for

119

example) does not involve the bodily feeling of being stabbed, but only involves having the *sort* of pain characteristically *caused* by a stab. On this alternative view, the stabbing quality of a stabbing pain is not an intrinsic property of the pain itself, except in so far as the adjective refers to the intensity or suddenness of onset of the pain. If the causal order of the world had been different, stabs might have characteristically produced pains of a quite different sort; for example, what *we* call a burning pain. And then what we now call a burning pain would have been called a stabbing pain.

However, this view is open to serious objections. It makes an adjective such as 'stabbing' too extrinsic a description of the pain, merely based on an association of ideas due to causation. If to call a pain a 'stabbing' pain is only to talk of the *cause* or supposed cause of the pain; then it ought to be possible, at least in theory, to characterize the pain *independently* of the fact that it is the sort of pain caused by stabbing. (The effect is logically independent of the cause.) Now how can we differentiate a stabbing pain from other sorts of pain (except with respect to suddenness of onset and intensity) save by using the adjective 'stabbing'? It does not seem possible to do so, and this suggests that the stabbing-quality of the pain is intrinsic to the pain. When we feel a stabbing pain, we feel as if we are being stabbed. (And I think it is irrelevant to point out that often, in actual stabbings, very little is felt at all.)

Another difficulty for this causal view is the problem of how we learn to associate the adjective with a certain sort of pain in the first place. We certainly do not wait until we are stabbed, and thereafter associate that sort of pain with stabbing. Do we immediately and instinctively find ourselves with the thought (which may or may not rise to a belief) that the cause of *this* sort of pain is a stab? This seems very unlikely. It is at least a simpler view to say that having a stabbing pain *essentially involves* feeling as if one is being stabbed. And so with other descriptions of our pains.

So it seems that very often the bodily impression that evokes the pain-reaction is quite determinate in character; an impression, say, of stabbing or tearing or burning. (The distinction between the transitive and the intransitive sensations is getting thinner and thinner as we go on.)

However, it must also be admitted that this only holds for *some* cases of physical pain. In other cases all we can say is that our bodily impression is of *some-thing-or-other* untoward going on in a certain place. This is peculiarly true of *aches*. We do speak of a *splitting* headache, but in general aches are 'blind';[1] we cannot describe them except by saying where they are and how severe they are. But in the case of 'blind' aches and pains we can fall back on the considerations advanced earlier.

## 2. HOW DO WE MANAGE TO CLASSIFY VERY MILD INTRANSITIVE SENSATIONS?

We pass on to a new difficulty. We have said that in the case of some pains our only bodily impression may

[1] To use an expressive term suggested to me by Dr. A. C. Jackson.

be that something-or-other untoward is going on in a certain part of our body. We have also said that some 'pains' are so mild that they arouse no pain-reaction in us. Now presumably we could combine these possibilities, and have a very mild pain that was also 'blind'. In the case of some other intransitive sensations, itches in particular, we have also said that our bodily impression is simply that something-or-other untoward is going on in a certain part of our body. And we could have itches so mild that they arouse no characteristic reaction in us. But now the problem arises: how can we distinguish between a very mild pain and a very mild itch (as we can)? According to our analysis, in both cases we have *nothing* more than an impression that something-or-other untoward is going on in a certain part of our body. This appears to make a very mild pain and a very mild itch identical experiences. But this is false.

Presumably, however, there is a physiological difference in the nervous stimulation that causes a very mild pain and a very mild itch. And it is not inconceivable that such differences of stimuli should have different psychological effects, even though they are insufficient to arouse the pain- and the itch-reactions. It might be that when pain-nerves are very mildly stimulated a bodily impression is produced, and with it the *thought* of pain, or the thought of classifying this impression as pain rather than as an itch, even though there is no pain-reaction. Or we could put the point by saying that even in very mild pain there is *some* reaction, *viz* the reaction of *saying* it is a pain, or of classifying it with pain and not itches. A very mild pain and a very mild itch would then be distinguished.

## 3. WHY IS NOT THE PAIN-REACTION DIRECTED TO THE REAL CAUSE OF THE PAIN?

The third difficulty is most easily developed in the case of pain. In normal circumstances the 'place of the pain' (that is, the place where something untoward *feels* to be going on) is the place where something untoward is *actually* going on. The pain-reaction is naturally directed to that place. In other cases, the 'place of the pain' is not the place of the untoward bodily happening, but nevertheless I am deceived, and *think* the 'place of the pain' to be the place where the disturbance is. Equally naturally, the pain-reaction is directed to that place. The situation is like that of a man whom I dislike because I believe he injured me, although in fact he did nothing of the kind.

But if I learn that the man had not injured me at all, and if this really had been the basis of my dislike, I will stop disliking him. But suppose I learn that the place where I feel the pain is definitely not the place where the trouble is. The nature of my pain-reaction does not alter in any way. I still feel the pain in the same place: it still *hurts* there. This seems to create a difficulty.

But two points may be made in reply. In the first place, our pain-reaction in such cases does tend to change in one respect at least. We have said that when we are in pain there is a loving concern for the painful place. Now if we know that the 'place of the pain' is causally unimportant, our attitude to it tends to change. We tend to transfer our concern to the place where the trouble really is.

But the really important point is this. The immediate

dislike that we have of physical pain is evoked simply by the *feeling* that something is going on in a certain place, and it continues to be evoked by that feeling, *whatever we know about the correspondence or failure of correspondence of that feeling to physical reality*. The bodily *impression* calls forth the pain-reaction. It is the impression that we try to banish.

If this is thought peculiar, we may consider a parallel case. Suppose we seem to smell a disgusting smell, but are later informed that we are victims of olfactory hallucination: that there is really no such smell present. It is perfectly possible that our *hallucinatory* sense-impression may continue to call forth *exactly the same disgust* in us, although we know perfectly well that there is really no smell to be smelt. It is true that disgust is a reaction produced by training, and one that can be removed by training, while the pain-reaction is more primitive and less amenable to conditioning. But this is a contingent difference, and does not destroy the parallel.

### 4. WHY DO WE STOP AT SENSATIONS?

On the view of the intransitive bodily sensations that we have been putting forward, such a bodily sensation is simply a bodily impression, although an impression that characteristically evokes certain attitudes in us. Now by perception we gain knowledge of the physical world: sense-impressions are generally only of practical interest to us in so far as they reflect the nature of physical reality. So in order to account for the (relative) incorrigibility of statements about aches, pains, itches, tickles, etc., we have had to assimilate them to statements about bodily sense-impressions, not to statements of veridical bodily perception. Now it may well be asked why, in this important field of perception, ordinary discourse restricts itself to sense-impression statements, instead of making perceptual claims about what is actually going on in our body.

Several reasons may be advanced. In the first place, we have seen that the reactions characteristically evoked by these bodily impressions are determined almost solely by the impression, whether or not it corresponds to physical reality. Since the reactions are an important part of our concept of almost all the intransitive bodily sensations, it is natural to talk about what feels to us to be the case, whether or not it is the case.

In the second place, the great indeterminacy often found in the bodily impressions involved makes it natural to forgo perceptual statements. We give little information when we simply say that something unusual is going on in a portion of our body.

Finally, as we have mentioned, illusions of bodily sense are, as a matter of fact, very infrequent. A visual illusion is a common thing, but the case of a 'phantom limb' excites wonder.[1] This means that, in the vast majority of cases, the place where the bodily occurrence feels to be, and the place where it is, are identical. Given the place of the pain, we are given the place of the trouble. (It is a recent medical *discovery* that many internal pains are not at the site of the trouble. Such discoveries have not yet affected our ordinary concept of pain, although they might do so in the end.) So

[1] Nelson took his 'phantom limb' to be proof of the existence of an immortal soul.

there is no need to insist much on the distinction between the place where the trouble feels to be, and its real place. And, as we have seen, where there *is* a discrepancy between the two, we do have *some* inclination to say that the real place of the pain is the place where the physical disturbance is.

This concludes my defence of the account of the intransitive sensations put forward in the previous chapter. A detailed account of each sort of sensation is niggling work, and I would certainly not claim to have elucidated every feature of our talk and thought about the intransitive sensations. And, in such a field, inaccuracies in what I *have* said are all too easy. But it may be hoped that the general lines of the theory are correct.

# CONCLUSION

So it turns out that all bodily sensations (whether 'transitive' or 'intransitive') are simply bodily sense-impressions, or, in some cases, tactual sense-impressions. Bodily sensations are a species of sense-impression. When we have a bodily sensation it feels to us as if something were going on in our body or as if something were in contact with our body: impressions that may or may not correspond to reality. We can give an account of bodily sensation in terms of the concepts involved in perception: no unique, irreducible, concepts are required. This is quite an important simplification in the field of philosophical psychology.

The so-called 'intransitive' sensations differ from the other bodily sensations in the relatively indeterminate nature of the bodily impressions involved, and the fact that (with some exceptions) certain reactions are characteristically evoked by the occurrence of the impressions. (Reactions which are built into the concepts of such sensations.) They are an *eccentric* sub-species of the genus sense-impression, and it is this eccentricity that has tempted some to regard them as something quite other than sense-impressions.

A further conclusion, of considerable philosophical importance, has emerged from the argument of this book in a more incidental way. In the course of the discussion of tactual and bodily perception and of the nature of transitive and intransitive bodily sensations, it has been argued that the sole immediate *objects* of bodily and tactual perception are the thermal and spatial properties of our own body, and physical objects in contact with it. Heat and cold, it was maintained, are the *only* 'secondary qualities' that we need postulate to explain tactual and bodily perception. Bodily sensations involve impressions of thermal and spatial properties only. This means that the list of 'secondary qualities' that the philosopher need recognize is a short and determinate one. Colour, perhaps light and shade, sound, taste, smell, heat and cold: and the list is exhausted. An investigation of the nature of the 'secondary qualities', one of the most difficult and important problems in modern philosophy, might be simplified by this preliminary ordering and reduction of the number of such qualities.

# INDEX

---